I Just Lately Started Buying Wings

I Just Lately Started Buying Wings

missives from the other side of silence

Kim Dana Kupperman

GRAYWOLF PRESS

This publication is made possible by funding provided in part by a grant from the Minnesota State Arts Board, through an appropriation by the Minnesota State Legislature, a grant from the National Endowment for the Arts, and private funders. Significant support has also been provided by Target; the McKnight Foundation; and other generous contributions from foundations, corporations, and individuals. To these organizations and individuals we offer our heartfelt thanks.

Published by Graywolf Press
250 Third Avenue North, Suite 600
Minneapolis, Minnesota 55401

www.graywolfpress.org

Published in the United States of America

ISBN 978-1-55597-560-9

2 4 6 8 9 7 5 3 1
First Graywolf Printing, 2010

Library of Congress Control Number: 2010920766

Cover design: Kapo Ng @ A-Men Project

For Dustin Beall Smith, who follows his bliss to the max.

And in memory of my parents, Dolores, Abner, and Phoebe, and my brothers, Ron and Gil.

I travel to places . . . Some would not be easy to find on a map, others would be.

John Berger, *Keeping a Rendezvous*

contents

introduction

Not that long ago, when there was no such thing as "creative non-fiction," there was essay writing and fact writing and biography, auto-biography, and memoir. The best of these were not distinguished by their creativity—it was assumed already, as a matter of course, that writing was a generative act—but by their elegance and clarity and allegiance to the essence of the human experience. Too often these days the words *creative nonfiction* are code for "sort of made-up." Too often they are a license for self-indulgence.

Kim Dana Kupperman's *I Just Lately Started Buying Wings: Missives from the Other Side of Silence* is notable not only because it is not sort of made-up, and not self-indulgent but, more important, because it returns readers to the fundamental nonfiction experience, an immersion in real life, exquisitely rendered. Here is a world—her world—so finely observed that it becomes our world too. Here is a voice, both smoldering and meditative, that inhabits every page like an attentive host, inviting us in and offering no choice but to step over the threshold. The pages turn, it seems, of their own volition.

Kupperman's is a voice we trust implicitly. It is unsentimental, undramatic, curious, wounded, poetic. And it is ballast for facts that might seem too awful or prurient or heavy otherwise. Suicides, drug addiction, adultery, custody battles, AIDS, and all the other modern plagues that supplanted the boils and locusts and killing of the firstborn of the Bible, are part of her story, yet none are the story itself. There is no question of blame, no recriminations, not even any villains, even in the face of very bad behavior. The mark of a writer in full control of her material, as is Kupperman, is letting the story tell itself artfully, but without artifice.

As a collection of what Kim Kupperman calls "missives"—think of them as an assortment of letters found bundled together—*I Just Lately Started Buying Wings* is anything but a straight-ahead narrative with a plot that arcs and resolves. It's episodic, more slideshow than movie. True, the girl in the third missive, whose parents use her like a piece of rope in a game of tug-of-war, grows up and becomes the woman in the other pieces, a seeker, a traveler, a woman at home in the world. Still, there's no attempt to put the pieces together, to invent causes (divorce or parental infidelity, say) for effects (a failed marriage, a passionate love affair). How we become who we are may be more mysterious than how we become. Kupperman's missives remind us of this.

Even so, most of us want to know how the story ends, even before it's over. We're curious about that little girl. How did she turn out? Though the answer is, no doubt, complicated, consider *this*—that is, consider this book you hold in your hands. Like its writer, it's got wings.

Sue Halpern
Ripton, Vermont

I Just Lately Started Buying Wings

missives from the other side of silence

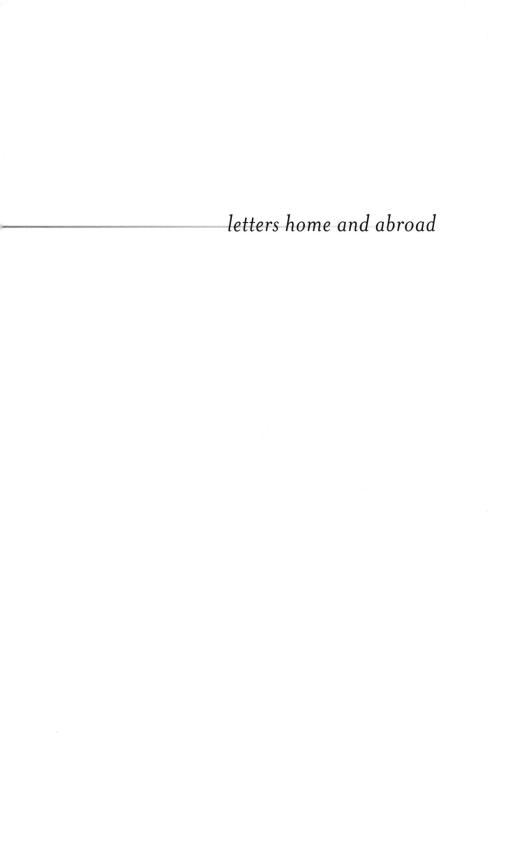

letters home and abroad

relief

Has it ever been absent, this desire
for every moment to stand in relief,
the unending row of them set
like solitaires into what passes,
burnished to unbearable depths?
    Melanie Rehak, "The Modernist Impulse"

I.

I woke to a downpour the March morning in 1989 when I had to identify my mother's body at the New York City morgue. Drenched, the
island of Manhattan smells cleansed, an idea of earth under all that
granite and steel and glass. When I opened my eyes, my bedroom
seemed fashioned not of four walls, but of small details. The shade
covering the window, a yellow number-two pencil in a cup, my address book opened to the *B* section—all these objects looked as if they
had been raised to a polish while I slept. In spite of the day before, the
day of my mother's heart stopping, of her two suicide notes, of waiting, and of possibly too much wine and definitely not enough sleep, I
could make out from my position on the bed the rip in the shade, the
eraser's rubbed-down edge, even the phone number for the city coroner penciled next to my mother's name.

I dressed and made my way downtown, toting an umbrella, identification, keys to my mother's apartment, all the necessary paraphernalia of a person attempting to fit into a world where the rules have suddenly changed. In the mezzanine of the morgue, I looked up to a large plaque embossed with letters that pronounced *Fiorello LaGuardia, Mayor.* Contemplating the possibility that news of LaGuardia's death forty-two years earlier had somehow not been communicated within this building, I felt the first trick of relief. I embraced the incongruity that you could die and still hold office, at least here where the city keeps the bodies of the unidentified dead.

The previous day I'd confirmed for the police, the paramedics, and the coroner that the naked body stretched out on the bed belonged to my mother.

"Yes, that's her," I said. Why, I wondered, had no one bothered to shut her eyes, wide open in terrified surprise? Her lips formed an elongated O, the shape of a scream I couldn't hear. She regretted her suicide, I thought, and was on the edge of dying when she realized her mistake. My mother had lived on edges—poverty, depression, having to be an adult before she completed childhood—and she died knowing their sharpness.

I was struck then by my mother's swollen feet, and in an attempt to relieve the swelling, I knelt on the floor and rubbed them. Maybe it was my guilt I was trying to rub away. Perhaps this act was simply the final performance of one I'd rehearsed throughout childhood on Saturday nights, when my mother and I would stay up late and watch old horror movies. The toes were almost too hardened to massage, the heels cool, the insteps stiff. As I massaged those feet, I knew it was the last time I would touch my mother's body.

After I'd talked to the police, I signed all the forms in which I acknowledged being the daughter of the deceased woman in the apartment. But because of a law about unattended deaths, I still needed to go downtown the next day to identify her body, and I resented this redundancy.

I stood on the wet floor of the morgue's lobby. Pouring rain outside. Folded, dripping umbrellas hooked over people's arms. The smell of drenched raincoats, the wads of tear-soaked tissues in pockets. Presiding over this frozen moment was Mayor LaGuardia, a dead man whose vital record, like my mother's, was incomplete.

The woman at the morgue placed a Polaroid head shot of my mother on the small table between us. I had imagined a more clinical episode, something you might see on TV—a walk down a corridor, a stranger peeling a sheet off the body, in a room of white tile and surgical steel. Instead, I sat in a small cubicle that was bare, save for a box of tissues and some chairs. Painted in a green that was neither sage nor olive, a color I suspected was mixed specially for institutions. A liminal zone between the announcement of death and its confirmation. A place governed by hidden people who typed memos, drank coffee, and washed their hands while I sat and stared at a Polaroid. The dead, separated from us by walls and photographs.

No one had warned me that the features of my mother's face had shifted, as though they had been moved to the right of the meridian defined by her nose. The O her mouth had formed only ten hours before had collapsed into lips that should have been parallel but were askew. I thought of all the years she had meticulously spent "putting on her face," only to wear a final version that disturbed the structure of her cheekbone and eroded the curve of her lip. What if I wasn't able to identify her? What happens to a daughter who cannot point with defiance and certainty to her own mother and say, "Yes, that's her"?

My mother's true identity was as foreign to me, I know now, as her face in that picture. She bleached her hair blonde, maintained an alabaster skin by avoiding the sun—who would look for a woman who was half-Jewish in all that paleness? To attract men she lined her mouth carefully with fire-engine red lipstick, but refrained from kissing lest it smear. She used wigs and powders and different colors with elaborate care. She even paid to have her nose broken and reset so that no one would notice that particular element of her Semitic heritage. My mother had spent her life mastering the art of disguise; she had learned to stand out to be concealed.

Perhaps the plunge into suicide had dissolved all that artifice and raised up the true design of her face, which seemed to emerge through the mask she had devoted so much time to fashioning. The face I saw in the picture was unforgiving, the cheekbones so chiseled they appeared stripped of the softness of flesh that I had relied on all my life.

Sitting in that room in the morgue, gazing at that head shot, a stomach-quickening uncertainty seized me. I barely recognized my mother's altered visage, and I craved the familiarity of her disguise. How could I say that her body, which was nowhere in sight, belonged to this image of a face that did not belong to her?

The woman at the morgue shuffled some papers. I looked up, but we never made eye contact.

"Yes," I said. "That's her."

Late October 1990. Three days before my older half brother Ron died, I contemplated sneaking into his hospital room and opening the morphine drip all the way. Instead I spoke awkward prayers to a creator I couldn't envision as I stood in a circle with my family in a hospital corridor on the AIDS ward, my head bent and eyes closed while a rabbi led us in prayer. How to petition God, I mused then, as somebody paged a doctor and people walked past us. I asked that my brother be relieved of his suffering. But my father and my brother's mother, I suspected, requested that he remain bound to them. Our prayers would cancel each other's, and then what?

When my brother died, he wore such a peaceful expression that I barely recognized him. His salt-and-pepper hair against the white pillowcase—the same curls that were drenched in sweat just several days before—seemed soft and clean. The sheet, which had before only emphasized his emaciation, appeared to caress his body and give it back its substance. During the last year of his life, my brother's face started to sink as his cheeks hollowed and his jawbone protruded. The creases at the corners of his eyes had tightened, squeezed out the laugh lines, and hardened into an expression of permanent anger, or perhaps remorse. It seems peculiar now to think that this man, who had raged his entire life, stopped raging when death approached.

I imagine that my brother welcomed death like a sentry who, relieved of watching for danger, succumbs to sleep. I like to think of him lifting off from the landscape of pain his body had become. Like the heron I once saw that unfolded its wings and levitated from the road. Gone, with just the slightest rustle of feather.

II.

Numbness alternating with dread gave rise to my inability to scatter my mother's ashes, and so they remained on a shelf in my bedroom closet for almost two years. Sometimes when I opened the closet door to reach for a dress or a blouse, the sight of the plain cardboard box containing the can of her ashes would freeze me in place. What kind of person keeps her mother's ashes on a shelf in the closet like a sweater that's too tight or a handbag that requires repair? I reminded myself that no sacred niches decorated the walls of my apartment. There were no shrines. No one had taught me the etiquette of ashes.

Since I wasn't planning on urns or a mausoleum, the closet seemed the most discreet arrangement.

Arrangements. This is code for everything that must be completed once someone dies—the repeated telephone conversation with family and friends, the wording of the obituary, the date and time of the service, the cremation and the memorial, the completion of paperwork, the transportation of the body, the disposal of personal affairs, the disposition of remains. In arrangements, though, there is a hint of relief, the kind that is brought about by busying away the grief until it seems to evaporate. "Wind blowing over water disperses it," says the *I Ching,* "dissolving it into foam and mist." After all the busywork, there is the accumulation of family and friends in one space (too small) and the never-ending food (too much). In this swell of comfort, you feel awkward and exposed, like the subject of an overheard secret. Then, those who have gathered disperse. You wrap and store the leftovers, wring out the sponge used to clean the counter, turn out the light on the fingerprints that linger on the refrigerator door. Later you touch and sort, discard or keep for another time all the artifacts that testify to a life that has passed—a tiny bear carved of jade on my mother's perfume tray, a fur hat on my brother's bureau that my father cannot wear but which fits me. Eventually all these objects are not only handled more than once, they are packed into containers, some resurfacing on shelves or in drawers years later, others given to friends, shipped off to the Salvation Army, or carried away to landfills. So many things we once thought were useful or beautiful dissipate or are buried, as if there was no point to having them in the first place. But in the act of letting go of them, there is a relief that they no longer have to be carried, cared for, or worried about.

Two months after Ron died, I moved to France, as if I were another artifact left behind after my mother's death, as if I needed to ship myself off to some place where no one would recognize that I belonged to her. But before I left, I made arrangements to scatter my mother's ashes.

III.

A freezing December day in the New Jersey suburbs where I have come to leave my mother's remains. Old snow and ice congeal into a slick mass that looks like gray enamel. I am with Laurie, my mother's goddaughter, whose deceased mother was my godmother, and whose ashes she has come to scatter. The bulk of our winter clothing and the nondescriptness of the almost identical canvas tote bags we've chosen for the excursion make me feel conspicuous. I am neither comfortable nor ill at ease standing in the backyard of the house Laurie grew up in, where my mother and I spent many holidays together. I am simply cold and slightly annoyed at myself for putting off a ritual that should have been completed sooner. The house is for sale, the trees bare. Laurie and I might be any two young women looking at potential homes, on our way from one place to another, bundled for winter. The reflections of our shapes seem pasted on the surface of the dark windows. It would be easier to be that temporary, almost liquid reflection of myself than to stand here shivering in the icy wind, ready to consign to permanency my mother's remains.

"Right here," Laurie says, pointing to two old trees. "We should scatter them right here, under these two maples."

I agree. In the fall, one of those trees burns yellow, the other red, just like our blonde and copper-haired mothers. We remove our respective cans from the bags. *Remains,* the stuff inside is called. Remains, I think, of women who orchestrated holiday lights, gifts, and party dresses. Women who presided over each year's variation on the turkey and pecan pie, twice a year within a month, every year. Women who said things like "Beauty hurts," and who taught us that birth control, blush, and bleach are essential for life as a woman. None of this is written on the plain tins. Nothing about how they had invented themselves with ordinary tools like eyeliner and lipstick. It seems a disservice to them both to be reduced to *remains*, packed into containers like small paint cans, without even a label like Butter Whisper or Adobe Dust. I wrestle briefly with the contradiction of remains as matter that does not remain still, but even my attention to this paradox drifts and settles, settles and drifts, until I focus on the practical task of opening the can. I fish around in my pocket for a quarter to pry off the top.

The lid doesn't budge.

"Do you think they sealed the can with superglue?" I ask, pondering the ubiquitous *they* and whether vacuum packing of ashes is standard procedure or some sort of funerary practical joke. The superstitious side of me warns that this failure to open the can is the result of having waited too long to scatter the ashes. *Maybe I'm wrong about remains not remaining*, I think. *Maybe if I don't open this can, my mother will remain with me forever.* I ask Laurie if she has a screwdriver. She doesn't. She tries to get the lid off and breaks a nail, which makes us both laugh until we cry, just as both our mothers would have done.

I work at the can for what seems like half an hour. Under all the layers of clothing, cold and sweat combine to bring new meaning to the word *feverish*. The stubborn quality of this moment is connected, I know, to my mother having the last word. Dolores was a woman who did whatever she could to be remembered after she left a room; she had at her disposal a plethora of disguises, from beaded Cleopatra-style headpieces to hot pants, and she was adept at telling stories about famous people as if she really knew them. After the sixth or seventh attempt to open the can, a surge of adrenaline spreads to my extremities, rushes down to my toenails, and out of my fingertips. One more pry with the quarter, and the lid opens, releasing a gasp of vacuum-sealed air.

&

Shock did not overcome me when I looked in the can and saw my mother's remains inside a plastic bag secured with a twist tie. Instead

I felt relieved by the plainness of it all, how the dusty grayness of the ashes obscured the Technicolor complexity of my mother when she was alive. An emptiness settled over me under the bare trees behind a house where there had once been light and children's voices, when Easter meant egg hunts and the end of December meant a new year was on its way.

I don't recall opening the bag to disperse my mother's ashes, or what I said at that moment, or if I said anything at all, but once the bag was emptied, I sensed myself as very light and small, almost invisible. Anchored to all things, yet hovering above the world.

My father has come to Paris, where I moved after Ron died, to scatter my brother's remains. His wife, Mary, grasps his left arm; on his right shoulder he carries a bag holding my brother's ashes. At the hotel, he unpacks.

The can with the ashes is still inside a cardboard box on whose surface my father's name and address are inscribed in worn letters. The frayed certified-mail form is still attached to the box. Before he came here with these ashes, was he unable to sleep, did he wander into the den—where Mary insisted he keep that particular package— and hold the box in his hands? I picture him absentmindedly rubbing his fingers over the name inked on the cardboard, as if that were not his name, and this box did not contain all that remains of his oldest son. I wonder if he ever questions what part he might have played in my brother's death, if he wishes he had been a different kind of father, one who watched his children more closely, or tried to understand how they felt instead of admonishing them for what they did.

"Take *that* home with you tonight," Mary says. She is unable to look at the box, to even say the word *box*. I consider her request, the whisper of despair in her voice. Then it dawns on me: what first-generation Jewish immigrant, raised in a kosher home, would feel comfortable with the incinerated residue of anyone, let alone a child? Into my black canvas satchel it goes. I take the Métro home with what is left of my brother, in a bag that now hangs from my shoulder.

Writing this now, I am unable to summon those faces from the Métro that evening. Perhaps I had cast my eyes downward, arms folded on top of the parcel in my lap. Maybe I was too tired to register any more information attached to this episode in my family's life. But if I remove myself from the story, I can see all the implications now: the father flies in an airplane and brings the son into heaven, the sister rides on a train and takes the brother underground. It is as if we were reenacting myths, carrying Ron in the same way to different destinations, one relieving the other of such obligation. There was my father playing at Daedalus, the maker of wings, the father of the son who would burn and fall. There I was, working at some version of Antigone, trying to ensure that her brother be honored beneath the surface of the earth.

My brother asked to have his ashes scattered on Mediterranean shores, but my father considers the request too expensive to honor, too complicated to arrange. In his final act as The Patriarch against whom my brother revolted, my father decides on the Normand coast-line instead.

It is raining—a June mist promising rain, really—when we take my brother's ashes to Deauville. This is the France of Camembert and apple brandy, of Henry James and Marcel Proust. These are the shores of D-day, and the birthplace of impressionism. Of course we are not here for any of that, but as we walk past the casinos along the grand boardwalk, I feel asthmatic ghosts beside me in the damp air.

We stand at the edge of a low, soft tide, the open can of my brother's remains at our feet. My father takes the first handful and casts the ashes to the sea. He is crying. As I curl my fingers around the dry, gray stuff, where life once was fleshy and brown, I notice a woman walking toward us. For a moment, I'm a little panicked. *What if she's patrolling this shore for people just like us,* I think, *people casting the ashes of the dead into the water?*

I point her out to my father, remind him that we have to be discreet. I replace the can's lid, close a tight fist around the handful of my brother's ashes, and thrust that hand into my coat pocket. When the woman nears, I see that her wispy, dark hair is greasy, and her black pants and jacket faded.

"Do you have a light?" she asks.

Do you have some fire? is the literal translation of this French query, and I realize she is holding a cigarette.

I want to laugh, the absurdity is so complete, the humor so apt to have pleased Ron, but I also want her to keep walking so my father and I can finish what we've started. As it is, I happen to have the light she needs, but it is in the same pocket with my closed and hidden fist. I reach around my back with my left hand to retrieve my lighter and light her cigarette. She takes a deep draw and exhales. I am relieved she doesn't notice my awkward movement.

"I simply love smoking in the rain on the beach," she says. She starts to walk away then stops, her feet just inches from the can of my brother's ashes, which she eyes.

"Collecting seashells?" she asks.

I nod. She smiles at me, continues walking. Funny, but I have seen no shells on this beach, no starfish or sand dollars either. Nothing that would stop me in my meandering along the shore and beckon me to pocket some proof I was here. And the birds are strangely absent too, even gulls. It is as if the scene in which I am participating occurs just above the surface of things, in a place where evidence becomes so light that it dissolves.

We had gone to that beach to leave something behind, not collect. The archivist in me felt obligated to preserve the moment, so I gathered its details. The woman's voice, which seemed to match the wispiness of her hair and the fadedness of her clothing. The almost impossible maneuver of lighting her cigarette. The dialogue. I did what I always do when faced with a potential memory: I chose the strangest part and cataloged its fragments.

"What was that all about?" my father asks.

Laughter would be a relief right now, but it would be inappropriate—my father would take it the wrong way and never forgive me. I explain to him without the slightest trace of a smile that the woman needed a light.

As soon as she recedes into the distance, I release my fistful of ashes. I watch the smaller flakes hover before they drift to the edge of the sea, and the heavier pieces fall directly into the wet sand. Suddenly all things water assume a cadence that contradicts my urge to laugh: the raised rhythm of the waves against the shore, the rain falling in fat drops, threatening to drench us if we tarry. The splatter, ebb, and flow suggest a flat seriousness that belongs to me simply because I am here watching the remains of my brother float in the water and disperse in the air. I am not too concerned that a fragment of my brother may have lodged in my coat pocket, tangled perhaps in a loose thread, his remains remaining. Instead I concentrate on emptying the can, and getting my father and me to shelter before we get soaked.

IV.

For most people, rainy days make for sad, dreary humors, and the cold evokes loneliness or melancholy. Movies and books are always using climate to suggest mood. Weather makes the metaphors in storytelling believable because atmospheric conditions suggest a character's temperament and provide context. What's happening in the heavens grounds us.

For me, rain and cold backdrop those moments when grief—that ache we carry underneath like a secret aquifer—suddenly subsides into a sense of relief. I'm not talking here of release from distress or sorrow: the relieved sigh when you finally finish crying, or the body's sag after days of weeping. Instead, I mean the relief of contrast, of projected or outlined edges—think relief map, or a bas-relief sculpture where figures rise out of a stone slab. Or, for me, the shiny Polaroid of my mother's face that surfaces each time I hear the word *morgue*. Or the city corner where I stood, transfixed by the sunshine on a building where my dead brother lay, the front of the hospital pushing out from all the architecture next to it.

In French, this idea of relief is expressed in the word *relever*, which means to rise again, to be raised. In ballet, the raising of the body initiated at the toes is called a *relevé*. This pressing up and onto the balls of the feet begins at the ground, spirals up the turned-out legs and hips into the torso, and lifts the dancer's head. Rising again, raised.

I like the idea that emotional rawness can suddenly sharpen ordinary objects. Amid the monotony of grief, everyday things—window shades, pencil erasers—stand out and help me find my way. Sometimes these projections manifest as an incongruity in the ordinary—a dead mayor who presides over the city morgue that holds my mother's body, or the woman who interrupts the solemnity of scattering ashes asking for a light, only to flick her own ashes away.

But perhaps it's the more subtle experience of relief as a kind of lifting up that most interests me. Relief lifts me up and lets me go—a daughter floats above the shadows while releasing her mother's ashes; a sister grips the edge of stifled laughter, suspended between the shards of her brother that drift in all directions. I observe as I participate, like those figures in stone that are both grounded in and raised above the slab. There I am, my feet firmly planted on the beach at Deauville, or on a frozen suburban yard in New Jersey, and there at the same time is my own absence, the shape of what is not there. Relieved of my weight yet holding on to it.

pregnant madonna scrubbing floor

Her name was Dolores, a prophecy of sorrows.

My mother is pregnant with me in my best memories of her. I have a photograph of her at that time, though you can't tell she's carrying a baby. She's sitting in a poolside chair, dressed in a black-and-white bathing suit, hands clasped on her belly, face framed with blonde curls. She smiles as one just roused from sleep—a soft-at-the-edges expression, lips parted to reveal the edges of her teeth, but not toothily self-conscious—and squints those sharp eyes, which seem to dare the photographer, my father, to release the shutter.

Maybe she was emerging from a good dream, one in which her appearance didn't matter. It's one of the rare photographs of my mother where she's not wearing makeup or sunglasses or a hat, and her hair isn't sprayed stiff into an updo of the late 1950s. She looks as if she might have been happy, and perhaps she was for that one instant when my father said, "Smile, Dolores." Of course the moment stretched into one minute—then three or four—as the man she had married fiddled with the camera and focused the lens, and the whole time, she had to maintain that smile, knowing vaguely that this interminable holding of the smile and the dragging out of the picture taking—of being the *beheld*—were precisely the kinds of things she'd say later were wrong with the marriage.

A tiny, only partially formed being, I float inside her, suspended in an amniotic flux where syllables are drenched in my father's voice and that original, unforced, and unheld smile works its way down to me from my mother's lips as a mild infusion of heat, as if she had bared her belly to the sun.

Half-Catholic and half-Jewish (and at home nowhere), my mother tried to bleach out that darker side and soften the angles with peroxide, strict avoidance of the sun, a nose job. But she couldn't change the deep peat brown of her eyes. If she were alive today, she would have used those contact lenses that change the color of your eyes. My mother, who once worked at Revlon, took the party line of the cosmetics industry—Why not change the things you can?—at face value, literally.

"Beauty hurts," she was fond of saying.

I wouldn't understand until after she died that men had harmed her because of her beauty. Or how she carried the pain of that hurt in the same way she carried me—because she had to—and that she carried too the pain of her mother and her grandmother, women whose beauty hurt. Eventually, because she could not change her belief in some truer identity made not of image, but of faith and love, my mother became as intimate with despair as she was with her reflection in the mirror.

Being beautiful takes a lot of time. Hair alone can consume an hour or two a day, depending on length and style. Then there's the perfecting of skin: masks, toner, astringent, soap, moisturizing cream (three kinds: morning, night, under the eyes), blemish control and concealment, hair removal or bleaching, lip plumper, and, for some, appointments with the plastic surgeon. Saline injected into the spider veins. Liposuction. A tuck here. A lift there. Scars at the hairline. Starvation or forced vomiting. Depression when the hair loses its shine, the skin its elasticity, the muscles their tone. Beauty that hurts.

But the day my father took the photograph, my mother sat in the shade, her hands resting on the belly that would harden, like a shell as I grew inside her, and there was only a pretty woman smiling—pretty because she was naturally pretty, and smiling because she was pregnant with the photographer's child. There was only her brief happiness, washing me in warmth as I floated.

My mother passed on to me (among other traits) her gift—others might call it an obsession—for cleaning. If I had been outside her womb the day before I left it, I might have seen her on her knees in the kitchen. I call this scene *Pregnant Madonna Scrubbing Floor.* The image seems so familiar to me, as if my consciousness had been allowed to transcend the border of my mother's uterus and hover near the ceiling or a wall.

If I could paint this tableau, the window would be washed in stark white, obscuring the ledge, the buildings, the city beyond it. I would place my mother's hands at the center of the composition. A wisp of her almost platinum hair would stray from the confines of a red headband. Cherry red.

With the sleeves of a man's pinstriped shirt rolled up past her elbows, my mother makes strong circular movements with a stiff, soapy brush. She wears only that shirt and black underwear. Her feet are bare, ankles puffy like fresh bagels. Her expression placid as a lake. Her lipstick—a union of tangerine and red curry—burns like an ambiguous fire.

In spite of the danger of truth and fire, she utters the truth to me for the first and last time that day.

"Clean makes true," she says.

With that annunciation, she rises from the floor, whale bellied, pink kneed, splashed with soapsuds. Her lips painted oracle red, full of proclamation. Afterward, until the day she died (and even after that), she teaches me exactly what it means to set one's house in order.

Scrub the floors. Remove dust. Make sure the dishes are washed and dried and put away. Clean the fridge at least once a week. Empty the trash. Keep a list of what is necessary.

In my vision of the pregnant Madonna scrubbing the floor, I am about to emerge from my mother and am restless; after all, she is restless, washing a floor she has probably cleaned five times in the last two days. Gone the softened smile of the woman in that photograph taken by my father. In its place, my mother's lips are tightened into a swollen line. She wants to get this birth over with, and though she's been through a lot of pain already—from the operations on her spine to the maintenance and consequences of a beauty that hurts to the ache in her back from pregnancy—she's unsure if she'll be able to handle all the pain she thinks will come flooding out of her when she delivers her baby. She suspects she carries a girl, and this belief overwhelms her: to carry on a tradition of hurt across these generations of women—her grandmother deaf and widowed at twenty-something; her mother dead at thirty-eight of multiple sclerosis; her own spina bifida and consequential drug addiction—it has to stop somewhere. Perhaps it is at that moment, on her knees, shirt wet, embracing every hurt she's ever known, that she prays her child will be the last in this line.

As she scrubs and rocks, then rises to empty the bucket of soapy water, I flex my limbs against her womb, push down and to the sides.

"Trying to kick your way out?" she asks. "You'll have to wait until I push you out."

I *am* trying to kick my way out, and I can feel the chill of her fear, how terrified she is of my urgent need to leave this place, my first home, and come up for some air.

When it is time for me to arrive, she does not, in fact, push me out. Instead, the doctors prepare her for a C-section: wash, shave, and anesthetize her. I know the medicinal wave is coming before she feels it, and I stretch my arms and legs out in her womb, bracing for its impact. The wave crests and I taste wild mustard and clay, smell olive trees and caves. I catch bits of these flavors and odors, as if they were pieces of some mysterious poem. The wave swells, crests, breaks, wells, and ebbs again, a cycle that will last until I am delivered. When it's over, I'll close my eyes and listen to her breathe. Or dream about what it was like when I floated inside her and the luxury of her voice read me poetry. Over forty years will pass before I remember how her brief, sleepy smile warmed me on the day my father said, "Smile, Dolores." As if he could coax happiness out of a woman whose name meant *sorrows*.

habeas corpus

The Secret File

My father gave to me what I have come to think of as the Secret File, the one I had requested for fifteen years, the one about my parents' custody battles. I was forty-five—the same age my dad was when I was born—when I finally opened the file.

"What you want is in the den closet," my father told me a week before he died. We were alone in his room at the rehab nursing home during one of those moments of impressive lucidity he enjoyed as his life waned. I knew he was talking about *the* file and could barely believe his stubbornness was melting. I nodded. It didn't occur to me that he knew he would die within seven days. When I returned to his apartment, I opened the closet door and found the bag, wedged between the wall and a carton, as if it were some kind of archaeological find that had, because of high winds or heavy rain, emerged overnight from the soil of a dig site. Inside were the court orders and transcripts typed on bond paper, secured with rusting brads and staples, and folders of other documents, bound with dried out rubber bands that broke when I touched them, the whole bundle of papers moldy because they had been stored in the basement of my father's Florida apartment building.

Somehow, before my father became so ill that he needed to be hospitalized, he had summoned the strength to dress, use his walker to leave the apartment, and take the elevator downstairs. He traveled seven floors to the lobby, and another to the basement. Maybe he conversed with neighbors along the way, or perhaps he rode alone silently, his mind making momentary departures in and out of the daily reality, though still he was possessed of a mind focused on the task at hand. He unlocked the storage room, a challenge as my father's hands had grown fairly useless when it came to keys or buttons or silverware, and carried the file, which weighed six pounds, a load for a man who could barely raise a spoon to his mouth, back to his apartment.

My mother committed suicide fifteen years before my father passed. After she died and I was unable to locate the court documents in her apartment, I started bugging my father to give me those papers, making requests whenever I saw him.

"Why do you want to read that stuff?" he asked each time.

"It's about my life. I have a right to know what happened."

I never told him that those papers had become in my mind the Rosetta stone to my childhood, that I had endowed them with such weighty magic because I have so very few memories before the age of nine. Certainly, the court documents would elucidate the past; maybe they would even evoke feelings that had gone unremembered. We never talked, my father and I, about how everyone wants what they feel they have not received from their parents. "No exception here, Dad," I might have said had I been thinking more clearly, or faster, had I felt able to be entirely honest with him, to say, "I not only want my memory restored, I want to know who you and my mother really were." It didn't occur to me that, having been himself a child once, in a family where secret keeping was as quotidian as bread, my father was quite familiar with yearning for something locked up and withheld by the adults known as parents.

Here's the great irony: the papers in the Secret File generate more questions. Court transcripts are like screenplays without stage directions: reading them, you have to supply tone and cadence, imagine the faces and body language of witnesses as they testified, speculate when and how glances traveled back and forth from the witness stand to the judge's bench to the large tables, and what those glances implied. Such speculation means resisting the temptation to fill in those details with scenes and characters borrowed from television courtroom dramas. And then there is the evidence entered as exhibits, things *not* in the file, invisibilities that complicate any truth that might be pulled out of the testimony recorded on paper.

You Must Have the Body

On March 5, 1968, my father's attorney filed in the New York Supreme Court a writ of habeas corpus and petition on my behalf. I was eight years old. The petition addresses my mother and demands that she appear in court.

The word *habeas* is the subjunctive form of the Latin verb *habere,* "to have." The subjunctive is not really a verbal tense, but a mood, and it suggests that the opposite of what is being declared is, in the mind of the speaker, also possible. Therefore, "You must have" is a statement that assumes the speaker is aware, or might suspect, that "You may *not* have." Such a writ sounds very dramatic: "We *command* you," the first line reads, "that you have the body of Kim Dana Kupperman, by you *imprisoned* and *detained.*" As hyperbolic as it sounds, as a legal instrument, habeas corpus is one of the oldest and most common remedies used to challenge the terms of child custody or visitation.

It was a good strategy. Because a writ of habeas corpus must be filed in a state's supreme court (as opposed to civil court, where most family matters are adjudicated), my father's attorney was able to bypass the growing pains of the then-young family court system, and avoid a legal arena where my father had no connections, and thus no favors to cash in.

Indeed, my mother had the body—mine, that is. And though *imprisoned* is not quite the word that captures how she treated me, she certainly detained me from seeing my father on a regular basis, and her "illness" (as she referred to the drug addiction that kept her bedridden) resulted in a fair amount of neglect. In my mother's apartment, the curtains were always drawn, windows closed, most lights off. Sometimes she was too "ill" and would simply forget to feed me.

I couldn't have been much older than four when I first climbed up onto the kitchen counter to eat dry, wheel-shaped noodles from the box. I can still see my hand reaching for the blue box with yellow letters and a cellophane window. *Ronzoni,* a word I could not yet read, but whose letters were a familiar design to my young eyes. I had eaten those wagon-wheel noodles after they were cooked so I must have deduced that it wouldn't matter if I ate them right out of the box. They tasted a little like paste. I had to hold them in my mouth, one at a time, until they were soft enough to chew.

On those days when Dolores emerged from her bedroom to play at being a mother, she combed the tangles out of my hair. In a photograph of one of those grooming sessions, perhaps taken by my mother's boyfriend at the time, maybe staged as evidence that she knew how to care for a child, neither of us appears happy, which may explain why such a picture was never entered as an exhibit at the custody trial. I face the camera, hands clasped against my chest, my head tilted to one side, my expression one that beseeches the photographer to *please end this* before tears occur. My mother is dressed in an uncharacteristic-for-her-taste *schmata,* a black bag of a house dress with white trim on the neck and arms, a garment that emphasizes her wan face and badly bleached long hair and hides the shapeliness that defined her. She concentrates on what must have been a Gordian knot of a tangle at the back of my head. Like Alexander the Great, who cut apart the insoluble puzzle with his sword, my mother once cut off all my hair after she could not pull a comb through it. I understood after that episode her power over my body, as I already understood her belief that "children should be seen and not heard." Because she could make me, or some part of me, vanish, I retreated and was silent. Looking at this image, I can almost conjure a memory—of repressed impatience on my part, frustration at my ingratitude on hers—to accompany it.

But, I wonder now, when my mother opened the envelope containing the writ of habeas corpus, did she find such language preposterous when referring to a mother and child? *Of course I* have *my daughter's body,* she might have thought. *I produced this body.*

My mother told me the story of my conception when I was about thirteen or fourteen, long after the custody fights had ended and I no longer lived with her. This was the period of my adolescence before *hate* became the primary verb I used to express my feelings toward her, when she dropped the pretense of mothering and tried instead to be my best friend. I don't remember doing homework on the weekends we spent together, though possibly the rule was to finish it Friday afternoon and review it for completeness upon my return home Sunday evening. The absence of responsibility meant doing as I wished, and my mother allowed me to hang out with my boyfriend in my bedroom with the door closed, smoke cigarettes and pot in the apartment, stay up late, things I was not allowed to do while in the care of my father and stepmother, Phoebe. We confided in each other, which mostly meant talking about sex, though the only story of her sexual exploits that she told was the one about my conception.

"Your father and I were in the Virgin Islands on our honeymoon," she started. I always loved that irony: my parents in a place whose name suggests anything but—though some might argue, everything related to—the celebration of marriage and the conception of a child.

"We were in bed, fooling around . . ."

I knew she was crossing a boundary by revealing something so private.

"'Say *fuck me,*' your father ordered. Well, Kimmie, of course I refused . . ."

Which I'm sure she did since my mother never swore.

". . . and then he said it again, a little more harshly. His face looked mean. 'Say *fuck me*, Dolores,' but still I didn't say it. Your father then slapped me . . ."

She lowered her voice a notch, and paused to light a cigarette, to let her story settle in. I felt both attracted and repulsed to what she was telling me, a rubbernecker at the intentional accident of my own beginning.

". . . he slapped me on the face. 'Say *fuck me*,' he yelled. He looked really mean. I said it . . . and you were conceived."

I suspect that some version of this story actually occurred and was afterward embroidered, such narrative embellishment having been one of my mother's characteristic quirks, and one more socially acceptable than her pathological lying. But no matter what really happened, that particular scene belongs to the private life of my parents. It is the kind of story that, after hearing, one might ask (or think), "What kind of mother tells her teenage daughter such a story?" And while this particular narrative didn't inflict on me any intense emotional harm, my mother knew that I would never forget it.

What I didn't—couldn't—realize when my mother told that story was that it would become a prescient preface to the hundreds of pages of court documents I would secure from my father three decades later.

At the Doll House
My father moved the Secret File from New York to Massachusetts, then Connecticut, back to New York, and finally to Florida. In the course of forty years, I'm sure he removed the contents—as he was wont to do with other personal files he kept—and examined them, reminiscing, allowing old anger to reignite, assuring himself that he had done the right thing. The bulk of the file consists of transcripts from a thirteen-month trial—initiated with the writ of habeas corpus in 1968—in which my father sued my mother for custody of me. Separation agreements, a Mexican divorce decree, affidavits and court

orders, and several pieces of correspondence between my father and attorneys constitute the remainder. Pieces are missing—transcripts from a seven-day habeas corpus trial in 1965, items entered as exhibits, receipts for what was disbursed to pay for these legal proceedings.

The file contains a report, authored in 1962 by a team of private investigators, which reads like a B-movie script of a marriage gone awry. Complete with a femme fatale, played by my mother, in an impossible marriage to a Jewish version of Fred MacMurray, played by my father, Abner J. Kupperman. July 28, 1962: three men known as J.M., A.B., and C.L. observed my mother as she arrived in a hired black Cadillac at an attorney's office on Madison Avenue. They followed her when she left the building with my father and accompanied him home to 300 Central Park West. A half hour later, they watched my father put my mother into a taxi, which she took to Penn Station. After purchasing her ticket for the Bay Shore train, she bought a candy bar and waited on the platform. One of the investigators followed her onto the train. The other two drove with my father to Bay Shore, where they boarded the 7:00 PM ferry to Ocean Beach, Fire Island.

By car, the trip to Bay Shore takes about an hour; the ferry ride to Ocean Beach another thirty minutes. At first I imagine them in suits, but then I figure that they probably opted for more casual, less obvious apparel—sport jackets, slacks, no ties. My father was forty-eight; the others I place in their late thirties, not from any evidence in the report, but because it feels right that my father should be the oldest man, that he should require the vitality of younger men to assist him in catching his wife—fifteen years his junior—at a game he regularly (but discreetly) played. They all smoked, though for my father, smoking meant a long Havana cigar, whose paper rings I coveted as a little girl. They traveled in relative silence on this trip—my father wasn't the kind of man who talked to strangers about his life, though I'm sure he wondered whether any of the findings would make their way into public light and chip at his successful career as a fund-raiser for Jewish philanthropies. The four men had come together to catch my mother in an act of infidelity. There wasn't a lot to say. Instead, my father probably made a clicking noise in the back of his throat while jingling the change in his pocket. The air smelled of salt and grass warmed by the sun. The man who drove removed his jacket and rolled up his shirtsleeves. The three of them bought tickets for the ferry, made their crossing without event, and settled in to watch "the subject," Dolores Kupperman.

At about eight thirty that evening, my mother emerged from her residence, wearing long white pants, a multicolored blouse, and a kerchief over her hair. She stopped at a dress shop and then proceeded to a cottage known as the Doll House. Several minutes later, she left with a male companion, one Manny Wolf, who held her around the waist. Another couple emerged from the Doll House, and all four went to an establishment called Goldies, where they sat at the bar until they were seated for dinner. At that point, the three investigators decided that my father should leave the island, to avoid any potential recognition.

"We'll go back to Bay Shore, Mr. Kupperman," said investigator A.B. "I'll go with you. We can take a water taxi."

At this point, I'm sure my father was furiously clicking the back of his throat, maybe even coughing. "Your mother lived in the gutter, Kimmie," he often told me, an assessment he likely formulated on that day in Fire Island, in the company of other men who, he feared, thought less of him for marrying such a tramp.

After dinner, the investigators observed my mother, Manny, and their two friends skipping back to the Doll House. After ten minutes, the other couple returned to Goldies. Ten minutes later, my mother rushed outside crying, rejoined the other couple at Goldies, and "sat on the lap of her blonde friend's boyfriend and joined the group in laughing and singing." At this point, investigator C.L. telephoned investigator A.B, who was probably standing by a pay phone.

"It's heating up here, A.B. Come back to Ocean Beach."

A half hour later, my mother left Goldies and returned to the Doll House, where Manny Wolf had remained. That's when my father and investigator A.B. showed up. The four men proceeded to the rear of the cottage, entered through the unlocked back door, and approached the bedroom, where they thought they would find my mother and her consort. My father opened this door while investigator C.L. "took a photoflash picture of the female subject, who was against the wall side of the bed, and the male subject, who was on the edge of the bed near the door." The four men dashed out of the cottage and took a water taxi back to Bay Shore, got into the car they had left there, and drove back to New York.

The report is typed, single-spaced, on two pages of bond paper. No letterhead identifies this document as having been issued by a bona fide investigation team, nor do any signatures reveal the names of A.B., C.L., and J.M. I find it curious that my father should have participated in the investigation. It occurs to me that he might have been alone, followed my mother, taken a blurry photograph, and authored the report himself. Or maybe his best friend, Mike, my godfather, was with him.

There are particulars in the report that would be whimsical if they didn't appear in material used to substantiate my mother's adultery. The purchase of the candy bar at Penn Station, for example. What *kind* of candy bar? Did she eat it on the train? I never once saw my mother purchase or consume a candy bar. Then there's the *Doll House,* Manny *Wolf, Goldies.* At any moment, I expect Ibsen's Nora to appear, dressed in a red cape and hat, with blonde hair. Looking just like my mother.

"You can't make this stuff up," a friend says to me after I call her and narrate this part of the Secret File. Never mind making it up, I have no idea what to make *of* it.

Other details provoke questions. The Madison Avenue address that appears in the beginning of the report is the same as that of my mother's attorney at the time. Maybe my parents had been discussing the terms of their soon-to-occur separation in that office. If so, it exhausts me to imagine the tension between them in the taxi home.

Assuming that my father really had hired three private investigators, I wonder how he acted, how he spoke to my mother as he helped her into the taxi that took her to Penn Station.

"Have a nice evening, Dolores," he might have said flatly, thinking, *see you later.*

Why was my mother crying after spending ten minutes in the bungalow with her supposed paramour? Maybe Manny Wolf told her he was only in it for the sex. What did the other blonde think when my mother sat on *her* companion's lap? *Go back to your own man in the cottage.*

No amount of research will unearth the thoughts of the characters in this moody drama. The only behavior that resonates as belonging to my mother is that she went out to "carry on," as my father put it, while someone else took care of me. Otherwise, this Dolores is unrecognizable. I rarely saw her eat sweets, nor did I ever see her as the kind of playful, affectionate-with-a-man woman described by the authors of the report. She never drank, save the occasional Brandy Alexander at a restaurant. Her gait was so slow I often thought of the line from Richard Brautigan's poem "like a turtle to his balcony" whenever I walked with her. She was too superstitious to skip.

"Don't step on a crack, Kimmie," she always said. "Or you'll break your mother's back."

A Shapely Blonde

A selection of newspaper articles, all dated April 8, 1958, also occupy the Secret File. The articles are about my mother. The only photographs of her in the folder are those reproduced in the clippings. Pictures she must have hated.

The headlines read: "Blonde Held in Attack On Ex-Suitor's Wife," "Woman in Wig Beats Bride; Jilted Blonde Salon Exec Arrested," "Charge Rival Beat Expectant Mother," "Housewife Beaten in Home by Woman," and my favorite (for the odd use of hyphenation), "An Ex-Girl Friend Shows Up. Arrest Blonde as Slugger." The subheads for this last article are "Entered Home Through Ruse" and "Pregnant Wife Reported 'Fair.'"

The photographs are possibly the worst pictures ever taken of my mother. In one, she frowns (and looks deranged because the photographer shot the picture from an angle slightly above); in another, she seems perplexed; and in a third, she weeps (eyebrows arched melodramatically) as she climbs the steps at the Fifty-fourth Street Police Station, her face and upper torso framed by the vertical spindles of the staircase railing, which might be mistaken at first glance for the bars of a jail cell. Her hair is short and tightly curled. She wears a horizontally striped coat over a dress whose demure collar is buttoned at the neck. Not flattering at all. No cleavage shows. Her demeanor appears puffy, as if her whole body had been crying.

The leads in four of the articles focus on her body: two start with the words *a shapely blonde*; the other two identify my mother as an "attractive blonde." She is also referred to as a "$20,000-a-year cosmetics firm executive." She looks like none of these descriptions in the photos. Only the *New York Times* article begins with the journalistic requisite of who, what, where, and when, lined up neatly without any tabloid fanfare: "A woman in white attacked an expectant mother on the West Side yesterday." Two of the papers report her age as twenty-six; three have it right at twenty-eight.

There is little variation on the actual story. A female assailant, disguised in a white uniform and a black wig under a green and gray head scarf—masquerading as either a nurse or a beautician, speculated one reporter—rang the doorbell of Isabella Neil's fourth-floor apartment at 345 West Fifty-eighth Street and asked to use the phone. Once she gained entry, the disguised woman beat the pregnant Mrs. Neil on the head with a hammer, concealed in her coat, which she abandoned in favor of a Mexican statuette in the apartment to continue her assault. According to one of the articles, after the incident, Mrs. Neil's husband, David, suggested to police that the perpetrator might be a woman named Dolores Buxton, with whom he had "gone around" for four years when they both lived in California, and who had sent him a telegram seven months prior to the crime imploring him not to marry Isabella. Detectives escorted my mother to Roosevelt Hospital, where Mrs. Neil positively identified her as the assailant.

The alleged crime occurred seven months before my parents' wedding. One scanty piece of evidence supports my suspicion that my father helped my mother out of this jam—a letter to an attorney dated February 1961 that refers to an enclosed $1,000 payment for services rendered on my mother's behalf. My father wrote, "I hope you will arrange for the formal dismissal of the matter at your earliest convenience."

I do not doubt that my mother married my father to appear more respectable in the eyes of the court. She met him the summer after the crime. He was well established in his career. He knew judges and legislators from his early days in politics, and was "connected" as the euphemism goes—through his best friend and early business associations in Newark, New Jersey—to players in the underworld environment. All I know of how my parents met is that mutual friends introduced them. My father was taken instantly, I'm certain, by the tall, sexy woman whose savvy mind grasped things faster than a bear trap. I have no clue how my mother convinced everyone of her innocence, though I vaguely recall a story she told about a woman using a wig to frame her for a crime, but that was long ago and seemed so preposterous that I didn't pay close attention.

The grandmother of a friend of mine always said, "Don't believe everything you read." As I was growing up, my father too insinuated that the written word is not necessarily gospel, perhaps because he carried a silent resentment toward the expectation of friends and peers to adhere to a people-of-the-book Jewishness. But his belief that truth might not always be in print makes me wonder why, when I was ten or eleven years old, finally living with him and Phoebe, and frustrating both of them because I didn't hesitate to voice my opinion that my mother was the coolest and best parent, he unlocked the filing cabinet and pulled out one of these newspaper articles.

"Here's proof," he said, "that your mother is unfit."

I was shocked by those black-and-white words into believing him. I didn't understand fully that *alleged* meant there was a possibility of innocence. The words seemed official because they were in a newspaper, and they served as a foundation for an allegiance to my father's version of my mother, which I wound up ignoring then embracing, ignoring and embracing. This cycle lasted until all three of my parents died and I held those articles in my hands, and because no adults were left to look over my shoulder as I read the words and studied the pictures, I was free to feel a small, but nonetheless reasonable, doubt in my heart. That's not to say that I don't think my mother was capable of such a crime; most of me—especially my intuitive self—believes she tried to kill that woman. My mother's innocence or guilt—like her mental and physical illnesses, drug addiction, and absentee parenting—was bound to be unclear. Everything about Dolores was enigmatic. Silly of me to think that once she died, and after I opened the Secret File, my ambivalence about her innocence or guilt would wane, or that the puzzle of who she really was would be solved.

It wasn't until after my father died that I sought the dossier, preserved as a matter of public record, of my mother's criminal case. The Recommendation for Discharge provides more details, including a substantial list of circumstantial evidence—a hammer with a trace of blood on it, found in my mother's apartment; an injury to my mother's finger, which Mrs. Neil claimed to have bitten and Dolores said was otherwise injured; contradictory stories told by my mother as to why she was late for work on the day of the crime. When Isabella Neil dropped the charges, she admitted that she was in "an exceedingly upset and agitated condition" when she identified Dolores Buxton from her hospital bed. But the real reason for the discharge was that the Neils, divorced not long after the attack, each "expressed a strong desire that there be no further prosecution." They told the district attorney they "did not wish to arouse the antagonism of the defendant," whom Mr. Neil described as "extremely unstable, vindictive, and potentially dangerous."

Appearances in Court

The transcripts of the 1968 custody case are voluminous—785 pages generated on seven days between March and December of 1968; another 112 pages devoted to a contempt-of-court hearing that started in May of 1969 and ended a month later. Three New York State Supreme Court justices, all dead now, took part in these proceedings. What little I know of these three strangers who intervened in my life—two men and one woman—I know from their obituaries, their comments recorded during the trials, and the decisions they made in my interest.

Thomas C. Chimera heard the part of the case that granted the writ of habeas corpus, ordered the Family Counseling Unit to evaluate the home environment, and moved the matter toward trial. Imagine having *chimera* as a last name. I wonder if the justice ever felt compelled to explain that the word for the fire-breathing, lion-headed, goat-bodied, serpent-tailed monster, which was supposedly the personification of snow or winter, originally meant "year-old she-goat." Perhaps he told his clerks—or maybe lawyers arguing cases before him joked—that his decisions were fanciful illusions.

Chimera was elected to the New York State Supreme Court in 1959, the year I was born. On March 20, 1968, the justice suspected he might not see the Kupperman custody case to its conclusion. "The matter is referred to the Family Counseling Unit," he stated, informing my parents that the issue would be decided after the social worker's report was received, either by trial or by stipulation. "Not necessarily by me because it all depends upon how long this is going to take," he added. My mother, who appeared without an attorney, was contentious. "I certainly understand English very well," she retorted when

Judge Chimera asked her if she understood that she would need to cooperate with the Family Counseling Unit, as well as submit to evaluations by impartial doctors and psychiatrists. When my mother uttered an under-the-breath comment about my father not having a "pertinent reason" for keeping me longer than what she said he had agreed to, Justice Chimera bristled. "Madam," he said, "if you are going to make a judgment for me, don't ask me to share my pay with you because I don't plan to do that. I am not making a judgment, and I am not going to let you make it either."

I would love to have seen how my parents dressed for their appearances in court. Unfortunately, court records do not inventory the clothing worn by plaintiffs and defendants. Maybe my mother used her cane—necessary, she claimed, because her legs buckled, but which more likely kept her stable while taking narcotic painkillers and provided evidence of disability for the city's social workers. Appearance meant everything to my mother, so I am curious as to what disguise she donned, which persona she attempted to elicit. Playing the role of Physically Disabled Single Mother, she might have worn little makeup, covered her hair with a kerchief, kept the colors subdued (a navy blue dress, tan overcoat, slightly scuffed flats), used a plain wooden cane. Had she chosen Former Salon Executive, her hair would have been styled at a beauty parlor and her lips colored a shade of red that hovered between seductive and severe; this Dolores would wear a Coco Chanel suit, eschew the cane for pumps and a matching alligator pocketbook. Or maybe she wore pressed brown slacks, an ivory silk blouse, and a tweed blazer, secured her hair in a French twist, kept the eye makeup in subtle mauves and lipstick a frosted pink, toted a leather briefcase, and used a brass-handled cane to portray Falsely Accused Former Cosmetics Industry Consultant, whose severe pain ended her marriage and career and was now threatening to terminate her parental rights.

My father probably dressed as he would have for the office, in a dark gray or blue suit, a crisp white shirt with *AJK* monogrammed on the pocket, and a silk tie. My stepmother, Phoebe, most likely wore something simple but classy, a pleated wool skirt that fell below the knee, a not-too-tight cashmere sweater over her pronounced bosom, Italian shoes with low heels. Justice Chimera wore a black robe.

A Body of Evidence

Francis J. Bloustein presided over the hearings between October and December 1968, issuing the final judgment in April 1969 that granted custody to my father. In 1968, almost two years after being elected to the state supreme court, Justice Bloustein found himself in a pivotal role during the three illegal strikes waged by New York City teachers that kept a million children out of school—including me—for thirty-six days.

When the writ of habeas corpus was served to my mother in March of 1968, I was living with her. However, there had been a period of fourteen months when she had handed me over to my father and Phoebe. According to my father, Dolores had said she was unable to manage me. In my mother's version of how she relinquished custody, she had informed my father that she needed medical treatment, hoping he would agree to look after me during her hospitalization. Regardless of who was telling the truth, after those fourteen months, my mother decided she wanted me back; she came to my school one afternoon in a taxi and took me home with her.

The trial started in October of 1968 but had already been on the docket five different times since March, rescheduled because my mother claimed her lawyer was incompetent. She knew this tactic would infuriate my father because he was paying an expensive attorney, and she probably hoped it would jeopardize Phoebe professionally since she had to take more and more time off from work to testify. On October 23, my mother tried to secure yet another adjournment, on the grounds that her attorney was not calling all the witnesses she wanted, believing that with their testimony she could not only outsmart my father, but make a good show for the court as well. She dismissed counsel, but Judge Bloustein requested the lawyer to remain by my mother's side—to protect her rights, he noted—as my father's attorney put in a prima facie case.

Dolores did not take no for an answer. She tried to argue with the judge, and though the transcripts do not describe her facial expressions, I can picture her clearly. Angry that things weren't going her way, my mother would have suddenly appeared taller than she was; her very dark brown eyes would have seemed hot if you could touch them. I had seen my mother morph into that larger-than-life rage, and it frightened me. If Isabella Neil, the victim of the hammer attack, had been in the courtroom just then, she might have said that her assailant had that same menacing countenance, that same molten quality to her eyes.

"Look, madam," the judge said, "I am not going to take dictation from you." By virtue of sitting on a raised bench, Bloustein towered over not just my mother but everyone else in the room, mitigating the sense of threat one party might have leveraged against the other. After asking that the Kupperman case be called, he addressed her again. "Sit down, madam," he instructed. "Give her a pad. She can make notes," he said to the bailiff.

Bloustein listened to the entire case. He read the reports from the Family Counseling Unit. He interviewed my parents. Of the three justices, he was the only one I met, when he summoned me to his chambers on my ninth birthday. I suppose he wanted answers, seeing, perhaps, that the adults in this case were overcome by their passions to the point of potential unreliability.

The day of that meeting, my mother woke me.

"Your birthday party is cancelled," she said.

"Why?"

"Your father has made arrangements for you to go to court today. He insists that you meet the judge. I'm sorry, Kimmie."

I believed her and she had me. Upset by this seemingly sudden turn of events, I was receptive to her instruction to tell Justice Bloustein how desperate I was to live with her; she even made me rehearse my answers. But I have no recollection of what I actually said to the judge. Matters discussed in chambers are off the record; the words I spoke that day are buried with Francis Jerome Bloustein. Of that encounter I remember only climbing what seemed like endless steps in front of the courthouse at 60 Centre Street in Lower Manhattan.

Francis Bloustein immersed himself in our lives over the course of five days at the end of autumn 1968. He listened to the testimonies of my father, Phoebe, and the parents of one of my childhood friends. He listened to my mother's witnesses, including a neighbor, her first cousin, her best friend (also my godmother), an ex-lover/business partner, a former babysitter, and a doctor. And Judge Bloustein heard my mother's version of things as well.

The attorneys asked questions intended to substantiate or undermine the credibility of my parents. Custody cases are trials of character really, and so my father accused my mother of being unfit, while my mother accused my father of lying. Phoebe was the only person who testified specifically about me, and in particular, she focused on the state of my physical and emotional well-being. She was a child psychologist and perhaps the most reliable witness in the courtroom.

Phoebe described a pitiful child.

"At age seven, she weighed forty-one pounds, exactly what she weighed at five and a half," she told the court. "She did not care to eat, or sit still, or sit and eat at the table. When she came to visit, her hair was frequently dirty and matted, underclothes torn and ragged. She picked at her body until it bled and scabs formed. She wet the bed every night, and was embarrassed. She was unwilling to bathe or brush her teeth. She didn't want to comb her hair. She didn't want to look in the mirror."

According to Phoebe's testimony, in first grade, I stopped up the toilets in school; the year these court proceedings started, I set a fire under the bed.

"When she came to live with us for fourteen months," Phoebe said, "Kimmie did not want to go to school. She stood in the doorway with her little hands on her little hips and said, 'I won't go.'"

At Christmas, she testified, I became agitated because of a card sent by a man who was the superintendent of my mother's building. I asked Phoebe if I really had to sit on his lap. "He's always trying to kiss me," I had told her. Though I do not recall the card, my memory of Jack Albrecht is clear. He wore cheap navy blue polyester pants pulled up high over his waist. His face was sallow, white hair cropped close to his skull, eyes sunken, lips pale. He always wanted to take Polaroids of me, which made me uncomfortable when my mother left us alone, and he took not one or even five, but twenty or thirty pictures in an hour.

When I was in my twenties, my mother told me that before he worked at the building where we lived, Jack Albrecht had been convicted of molesting children. Dumbstruck, I never asked her why she ever left me alone with him. I knew by then that she was unable to answer such a question.

"It was impossible for anyone not to see that this child was deteriorating," Phoebe told the court.

"Strike out *deteriorating*," Judge Bloustein ordered. I like to think he said this against his own good judgment, that his voice was softer than usual. But the word is still on the page. I was deteriorating, failing to thrive. It exhausts me just to think about who I was then, a child retreating from life, who looked like she never slept or bathed or ate with any regularity. A daughter who was frantic and afraid, yearning for maternal supervision and guidance. I do not remember being that little girl, but I recall wetting the bed. And although the judge ordered the word *deteriorating* to be struck from the record, how could he—a jury of one, the decision maker—have ignored its utterance?

Phoebe was the best witness my father could have had. She had saved notes I wrote to her, drawings I made, and a story I authored about a rabbit chased by dogs and hunters but who felt safe at home. These were all entered as evidence.

"In my opinion," she said, "this story expresses Kim's feelings." The justice did not strike from the record this subjective observation.

Phoebe also produced a list I had made. My mother objected, claiming it was not my handwriting, but when Phoebe testified that I had written the list on New Year's Eve, in the presence of my father, grandmother, and herself, the judge allowed it to be entered as an exhibit. In the list, I identified how I felt about my family. My mother was not mentioned.

"Did anyone ask her to do this?" my father's lawyer asked.

"No," Phoebe said. "She always sits and writes and draws."

When I was barely twenty, Phoebe gave me a drawing I had made at age six, an artifact that she did not submit to the court, but saved for when she thought I would be mature enough to make use of the information she planned to impart. On a piece of my father's note stationery—with *Memo from Abner J. Kupperman* printed at the top—I had drawn a girl with a forced smile and oversized hands in the middle of violent scribbles.

"She has no feet," Phoebe pointed out. "You must have felt trapped, that you could not escape the danger."

The miniature versions of who we become as adults are always available, if we pay attention. As soon as I could write, I made lists and stories. And before understanding the power of words, I drew messages.

Because my mother did not have an attorney for that first day of the hearing, my father, Phoebe, and two of their witnesses took the stand and testified without being cross-examined. Three weeks later, my mother brought a lawyer named Sidney Koblentz. I imagine him as a lunchtime Scotch drinker (straight, no chaser), with a taste for beautiful women, fast cars, and expensive suits. He attempted to undermine Phoebe's credibility by using her professional credentials to undo her testimony.

"Mrs. Kupperman, in your occupation as a child psychologist, isn't it a fact that young children frequently object to bathing?" Koblentz asked.

"Yes."

"Isn't it a fact that it requires considerable urging for children to brush their teeth regularly?"

"Yes."

"What causes bed-wetting, or is it a natural thing with a child?"

"It can rarely be physical, but it sometimes is. Bed-wetting is a psychogenic symptom," Phoebe answered. My father's lawyer probably saw what was coming. Attorneys who spend many years arguing custody cases must have an ear for this sort of testimony.

"Well, it is not an unusual condition for children of the age of seven or seven and half years, am I correct?" Koblentz asked.

"I don't know the statistics on it, but I would say it was fairly unusual. Enuresis can come from a number of problems in children that age, but usually there is some psychogenic problem that accounts for it."

"It could come, of course, from separating a child from its mother, could it not?"

"There is a possibility that this could happen, yes."

Here my mother might have leaned back in her chair, scoring a silent victory, appearing a little taller. Phoebe might have looked then at my father, an apology pulling down the corners of her eyes and mouth, an expression that only he could translate. Koblentz was relentless. He went after the part of her testimony about my weight. I wonder if he knew that Phoebe struggled with her own weight, and if he did know, if it was because I might have told my mother that Phoebe was often on a diet.

"If two parents were of a slim or slight nature or stature, it would be conceivable that their child might also be of a similar nature?" my mother's attorney asked.

"Yes."

Then he questioned her intent to raise me "in the Jewish faith," and if, because she was no longer able to bear children, that was why she urged my father to seek custody of me. He even asked her if, in the context of her work with the Child Guidance Bureau of the City of New York, she knew the psychiatrist who evaluated my mother in connection with the hearing. There were no questions from Mr. Koblentz about Christmas cards from strange men, or about the lists, stories, or drawings previously entered as evidence. He based his entire cross-examination of Phoebe on innuendo. That struck-out word, *deteriorating,* must have lingered, even in a sleazy lawyer's mind, as an apt professional opinion, one surely confirmed by the social worker's report, a document alluded to during the hearing, which only Judge Bloustein was permitted to read, and which I will never see.

At my mother's behest, Koblentz called six witnesses. Two of them—her best friend (my godmother) and her ex-boyfriend—were caught in lies when cross-examined. The doctor who took the stand also did Dolores more harm than good, describing a woman whose opiate addiction was not only registered with city officials but also not likely to cease. The physician probably felt lucky not to have his medical license revoked as my father's attorney uncovered one contradictory story after another.

Koblentz used a strategy informed by what my mother related as the truth. Her drug addiction (the primary reason offered by my father's counsel for her unfit mothering), she maintained, was due to legitimate pain caused by multiple operations necessitated by the congenital birth defect spina bifida. Her chronic pain, along with residual back problems, constituted the basis for her state-certified disability. When Koblentz put my mother on the stand, he started with questions about her medical conditions, questions she was able to answer with authoritative vocabulary and ease.

"Congenital spina bifida is an opening on the spine," she explained, very soon after being sworn in and taking the stand. "Mine was located on the first, second, third, fourth lumbar areas, which means from the waist to the coccyx. That means at birth there were no vertebrae in the first, second, third, fourth vertebrae areas."

"Did there come a time that you underwent surgery as a result of this condition?" Koblentz asked. Here, I'm sure, his voice is softer, his diction slower, than when he cross-examined Phoebe.

"Yes."

"And what procedure was used, if you know?"

"I know very well," my mother said. "They took the tibia from my right leg and used that as a donor graft for my spine and I was told at that time that this was the first of a series of fusions to fuse the spine completely."

Almost 30 percent of my mother's testimony focused on her body. I read these pages, comparing what she said with the autopsy report, which describes major scars and thus confirms the first surgery, but not the subsequent five operations she testified to have had in conjunction with her spina bifida. I spend time researching surgical procedures used to treat spina bifida in the mid-1940s, only to come up empty-handed. Besides, I finally conclude, what difference does it make if my mother had one or five operations? The pain was real to her, and it was coupled with deep emotional turmoil; she self-medicated. Certainly, she was not the first or last in my family to have made such a choice. Koblentz never asked her any questions concerning the condition of *my* body, an omission that suggests he suspected she would make a lousy witness because she was such an absentee parent. The point of her testimony about hospitalizations and surgeries was to prove not only that she required opiates to alleviate chronic pain, but that my father was aware of her medical condition and simply did not care that she suffered or required intervention.

The Quality of Mercy

Justice Margaret M. Mangan presided over the four appearances in the spring and summer of 1969, when my mother was charged with contempt of court after failing to return me to my father after her weekend visitations. In 1932, Margaret Mangan was one of the first women admitted to the New York Bar Association. In 1967, she made headlines when she ruled that a husband could not receive alimony from his ex-wife. "A husband who looks to his wife for support is placed in an unnatural relationship," she wrote, though she herself had never married.

My mother might have thought some bargain could be struck—here was a single woman, a Catholic too, sitting on the bench, and there was my mother, a single mother, half-Catholic, pleading for the return of her only child. But it didn't work out that way. Justice Mangan, whose penchant for children's safety was underscored when she ruled that landlords, not tenants, were responsible for installing window guards in New York City apartments, was more interested in my welfare than in forming an allegiance with Dolores Kupperman, though after the third violation of the custody agreement, the judge still did not wish to punish my mother for contempt of court. "Your little Kim is the ward of the court," she said, "and I am in a superior *in loco parentis* role with respect to [her]." Though she had no children, the judge did not hesitate to give my mother some parenting advice. "If parents only knew that children don't love; children *receive* love. That is the nature of children."

My mother must have burned inside hearing those words, issued by a woman who also said, "Power speaks and does not have to explain." Perhaps that is why Dolores disobeyed Judge Mangan and orchestrated my faux disappearance five days later.

I recall very well the Sunday evening in May that caused my parents to stand before Judge Mangan for the fourth time. My mother informed me that I would not be returning home, but staying with her. She took the phone off the hook and instructed me to leave it that way. "Your father will come here tomorrow and ring the doorbell. You are not to answer it, you are not to make any noise."

By then, I had seen the rage that transformed my mother's face and I knew not to disobey her.

"If you want to live with me, you must do this. And you do want to live with me, Kimmie, don't you?"

I nodded yes, though I knew her plan was all wrong, that my father would somehow find out, and that she was making me do something untruthful that I did not want to do. I was afraid at that moment to say no. If I could have seen then what is now evident to me, that she had manipulated me to believe I wanted to live with her, I probably would have obeyed her anyway.

"When you see your father, you'll tell him you were dropped off in front of his building, but instead of going upstairs, you took the bus and went to your friend Gabby's, where you hid in her bedroom."

That evening, my mother and I rehearsed the story she had invented.

"Where were you Sunday night?" she asked

"At Gabby's. She hid me in her closet."

"Why didn't you go to your mother's?"

"She wasn't there; she went to New Jersey on Sunday."

"Usually your mother waits in the lobby until your father comes down to get you. Why didn't she wait there this time?"

"Her friend Vivian said she'd give me a ride. She let Vivian take me to my dad's."

"Say *father's* instead."

"Vivian took me to my father's. But when we arrived, there was no place to park so I got out and told her I'd be OK. . . . Is that better, Mommy?"

"Why didn't you go upstairs when you were dropped off?"

"Because I want to live with my mother. . . . Right?"

"When you talk about me, say *Mommy*."

"Because I want to live with Mommy."

The next morning, my father came and rang the bell, banged on the door, called my name. My mother watched him through the Judas hole until he left, shuffled down the hall in her slippers, and went back to bed. I spent the day in front of the television, and when my mother didn't get up to make supper, I quietly left her apartment, went to Gabby's, and called my father. He arrived in ten minutes.

I want to remember feeling remorse for worrying him, but I was too focused on telling the story my mother had made me rehearse, too busy quashing my feelings with a narrative that I knew my father would not believe.

"Where have you been? We've been worried sick about you, Kimmie," he said.

"I . . . Vivian took me home . . . because Mommy went to New Jersey." I looked at the black-and-white floor in the hallway, willing the story to my lips. "Vivian couldn't park so she dropped me off and . . . I want to live with Mommy so I got on the bus and came to Gabby's and hid in the closet."

"What bus did you take?" he asked. I looked up.

"The one that crosses the park."

"Where did you get on the bus, Kimmie?"

I was caught. I had no clue how to answer. I started crying.

"It's important that you tell the truth, sweetheart," he said, taking my hand and leading me out of the building and to a waiting taxi.

My mother's attempts to prove that I wanted to live with her only irritated Justice Mangan. "The Court doesn't make idle words," the judge said at the June hearing, where she found my mother guilty of contempt and punished her by ordering visitation in my father and Phoebe's apartment. I see her making eye contact with my mother. "The quality of mercy is strained," the judge continued, "so that I look upon this merely as a violation of a directive of a Court that was sympathetic to Mrs. Kupperman when the third visitation was violated, but the fourth violation, there is no excuse."

The quality of mercy is strained. Certainly, my mother was shamed; she had stretched the judge's patience and burnt a bridge. Dolores would attempt some months afterward to mount an appeal, an endeavor she eventually relinquished when she realized that I was thriving in my father and Phoebe's care and was liberated from her gravitational hold.

On page sixty-five of the 1969 transcripts, my father's attorney introduced a letter into evidence. My father explained that I wrote it as an apology for having lied about where I was when he was ringing the doorbell that Monday morning. I do not remember the relief that surely ensued when I finally told him what happened. Nor do I recall the punishment he would later describe for the court: no television or phone calls for three days, which he said I tried to get out of by writing the apology. My father stood firm; there was no deal making where a lie was concerned. I wrote the letter anyway, and I found this note preserved with the records in the basement of 60 Centre Street. "Dear Daddy," I wrote in a shaky, troubled script with no resemblance to my present-day controlled and calligraphic print, "I told you a lie and I'm sorry. I won't tell you anymore lies [. . .] I am sorry I did not come to the door when you were ringing. But Mommy wouldn't let me. I love you both."

Almost ten years old, and already I understood that an act of writing might alleviate guilt, help me work out some interpersonal problem, or make peace, if not with someone else, at least within myself.

There was a second letter discussed before Justice Mangan. My mother testified that I had sent a letter to the judge, explaining that my father had forced me to sign a letter stating that I was in my mother's apartment from the Sunday to Monday in question. Of course, Margaret Mangan never received such a letter, and though my memory is incomplete, I am willing to swear that this particular missive was another of my mother's many fictions.

For Five Dollars and a Lollipop

The Secret File did not, as I had hoped, fill in the blanks of my memory. The court transcripts only illustrated how frenetic my childhood was, and how my parents reacted to that chaos. They were normal only in their complexity, and so caught up in bitterness and anger that the determination of my upbringing became a matter for the court to arbitrate. My mother didn't decide to perjure herself to keep me; she came to the hearing a chronic liar and was caught, though she never admitted that her lies had anything to do with losing custody of me. Her lying, I believe now, was not the product of malevolence, but a survival strategy used to cope with some trauma that I will never identify or confirm, no matter how many files I unearth. She believed the truth would harm her. And there was the pathology of her drug addiction, for which lying is requisite. My father wasn't a paragon of truth either, but he was well practiced at appearing virtuous, able to conceal his more unsavory behavior from public scrutiny (he was a compulsive gambler who happened to have business connections in or near Las Vegas) or to mask it in social convention (he married six women, disguising, he thought, his penchant for what his third wife—who outlived him—bluntly called his "womanizing").

My mother detained my body for a while. When Dolores was no longer able to adequately care for me, she was forced to surrender my body to my father. And that is what I remember most about the custody hearings, an incident I call The Exchange, when I was taken to my pediatrician's office and handed over to my father.

My maternal grandfather, who hated my father almost as much as he disliked his only daughter, flew to New York at my mother's request. He was to meet us at Dr. Stone's office. That morning, as I dressed, my mother coached me. "As soon as your father tries to leave, start screaming that you want to live with me. Throw a tantrum."

"OK, Mommy."

"If he picks you up, kick. Keep screaming." I nodded.

We took a taxi. I liked Dr. Stone. His bald head shone, he talked in a soft voice, and, after giving shots, he handed out lollipops. My mother and I arrived in time to spend several minutes alone with my grandfather, whom I seldom saw. When my father came through the door, my mother's father stood up, posturing.

"Sit down, Buxie," my father said to my grandfather. "Don't get in the way of this. It's not your business."

My grandfather puffed his chest, tugged at his jacket, and smoothed his hair with the heel of his hand.

"Good-bye, Kimmie," he said, looking down at me. "Here's some money, kid." He gave me a five-dollar bill, a fortune.

I was stunned. My mother glared at me.

"I don't want to go . . . ," I started. She kept glaring. "I don't want to go," I repeated, a little more vehemently. "I want to live with my mommy." My throat was dry. At that moment, Dr. Stone entered the waiting room, waving a lollipop. Cherry, my favorite.

My father reached for my hand. I held back.

"Come on, sweetheart," he said. I searched his face for signs of anger, but all I saw was a handsome, familiar face that I liked. Still, I shook my head no, clutching the lollipop in one hand, the five in the other. "We have to leave," he tried again.

"I don't want to go. I want to live with Mommy," I yelled, surprising Dr. Stone and myself.

He picked me up. My mother gave me that molten-eyed look that my grandfather, in a rare telephone conversation with me, would describe a decade later as how to identify a psychotic person. "When you see that look," he said, "walk the other way. And you know what I'm talking about because I was there when you first saw it, kid."

I started my pretend tantrum, screaming that I didn't want to go, flailing my arms and legs all the way out of the office, in the elevator, and on the street.

"Take it easy, sweetheart," my father implored. He set me down. I started crying, for real.

He hailed a taxi as I sobbed. Once we were inside the yellow cab, he gave me his handkerchief. I fingered the raised threads in the *AJK* monogrammed on the washed-soft fabric and watched the city streets pass by in a blur of tears.

We were stopped at a light when he said, "I'll take you to Rappaport's and buy you a toy."

That's all it took.

anatomy of my father

On a drive south in late July of 2004, I call my ninety-year-old father
from a rest stop in upstate New York.

"I'm just outside of Port Jervis," I tell him. *Jervis,* I think, *rhymes
with nervous.*

"Port Jervis," he says. "We used to go swimming there."

I'm amazed at his memory, which has been shape-shifting recently,
stalled out in the past tense of his life more often than not. End-stage
renal disease has defined my dad's life for the past two years and he's
reached the end of his prognosis. The memory loss is not from age but
from dementia related to kidney failure. *Try having all your blood taken
out and replaced in one day and see how that affects* your *mind,* I want
to say to my brother Kyle, who, in spite of all he claims to know about
medicine and renal disease, is alarmed at our father's drifting in and
out of decades past.

"When was that?" I ask.

"When I was a kid, of course. Port Jervis. What are *you* doing in
Port Jervis?"

How to answer without saying the obvious, that I'm on the road
to a different life, headed to a new job in Gettysburg, Pennsylvania,
780 miles away from a house, a husband, and the coastal Maine community where I've lived the last eleven years, a place astonishing for

both its wild beauty and severe economic poverty, a place I've loved deeply but where I can no longer remain.

Or maybe I should lie: Dad, I'm here in Port Jervis because I wanted to see where the states of New York, New Jersey, and Pennsylvania converge, and where the Delaware and Neversink rivers meet. Because this place was once called Magagkamack (alternately translated as "pumpkin field" or "land covered in grass") by the Leni-Lenape, and I like pumpkins as much as grass-covered lands. Because the Upper Delaware River is beautiful and eagles nest here and because this small town of ten thousand is home to a stationery company that made a biodegradable pen out of corn. Which reason should I give my father for being in a place I'm just passing through?

"Dad . . . ," I start. *In Port Jervis we were impervious.* "I'm on my way to Gettysburg."

"I *know* that," he says. "I asked what you were doing in Port Jervis, not *why* you're there."

He'll live another twenty years, prognoses be damned! He'll show them, those doctors and their predictions.

"I'm stopping here, to call you and let you know I'm OK." Even at almost forty-five, I am, from my father's perspective, still his little girl. We play a curious game, one I'll surely miss once he's gone. It works like this: whenever I'm traveling overnight, I phone him upon arrival at my destination and again upon my return home. But should I make a several-hundred-mile round trip in one day, or into town on icy roads or in a blizzard, I don't tell him. I just go. And pray I'll return in one piece and not have missed him if he called.

"Port Jervis . . ." His voice has the cadence of a man unable to say why he's lived this long and is remembering—now—this one thing. "We went swimming there when I was a boy. It was good to get out of Newark when it was very hot."

A muggy evening here in Port Jervis. Moths flutter under the fluorescent lights of the rest stop and fireflies blink on and off amid the grasses. I've never heard the swimming-in-Port-Jervis story. An entire piece of my father's life, this one eighty or so years old, dredged up because I happen to have stopped here. I feel a certain success at having called. I've collected information that wasn't part of the family chronicle until now. But when I return here several years after he dies, I won't be able to find where it was he swam. I'll wonder if he had it right, thinking *this* place was the one he knew as a boy, or if the town has changed so drastically as to be unrecognizable to him. Eventually I'll stop wondering, and Port Jervis will, for me, resemble neither the destination my dad pictured as he told me about his visits here, nor the depressed little New York community on the Upper Delaware I passed through before and after he died. Rather, the town will simply be a place in between one life and and the next, a place in our family's archive that is neither forgettable nor memorable.

My Father's Hands

My father died a month after that phone call from Port Jervis, in Broward County, Florida, just a block away from where he had lived for seventeen years. He lay dying on the critical care unit, a ventilator tube jammed in his mouth, his white hair in disarray. He resembled a creature more equine than human, his mouth contorted, open for inspection. *All those fillings,* I thought, *his teeth in good repair, a measure of good health. All that, all done now.* He had the teeth to chew but kidney failure prohibited him from eating everything he loved—frankfurters, melons, salt. Especially the salt.

"I learned how to cook with salt," Mary had told me many times during the two years my father was on dialysis. The last of six wives, she learned to cook the special renal diet, prepare the kind of dishes that did not belong to the culinary repertoire of an Ashkenazi Jewish mother.

"It's no matter," she told me. "Your father has lost most of his appetite; nothing appeals to him anymore."

Besides, as she and I both knew, the weakness in his hands made it nearly impossible for him to lift a fork. Never mind using a knife to cut a steak, or a spoon to scoop out the flesh of a cantaloupe. Even the saltcellar eluded his loose grip. *All that all done now.*

I mythologized the color of my father's eyes. The pale green of a glacier, and though filmy, his eyes still evoked ancient ice, even so close to death. I knew he saw and recognized me, and for one moment he seemed able to see something else—maybe something about me that no one else had ever seen, more likely something completely unrelated to me, like where he was going once his body failed him completely or how he was going to get there, and anyway what really matters is not the unnamed thing he saw, but that we looked each other in the eye. Our eyes became hands, and he did not let go. So strong, the grip of his glacier green eyes.

I tickled his forehead as he used to do when I was a girl and I didn't feel well and couldn't sleep. His hand was large enough to cover my face and his manicured fingers grazed my forehead as if he felt simultaneously afraid of and overjoyed by the simple intimacy of a man comforting his only daughter.

As a child, I never considered the things my father's hands had touched: money, his own body parts, pens, guns, piano keys, hardware, women's breasts (including my mother's), crap-table dice, the clarinet he tried to learn to play but then abandoned, an instrument he cleaned regularly until he sold it.

"Why don't you play anymore, Daddy?" I asked once when he opened the case. I was ten.

"I don't have time, sweetheart."

He assembled the smooth black parts and played one note. The sound reminded me of Canada geese.

"Benny Goodman I'm not." My father laughed. He pulled apart the sections of the clarinet, wiped them with a chamois cloth, and placed them carefully into snug compartments lined with cobalt velvet. Perhaps the feel of the clarinet's burnished black wood and the satisfying corked fit of one part into another appealed more to my father—who as a child had labored at the piano under orders from his mother—than the practice required to play an instrument. So he learned to clean, assemble, and disassemble it instead, and that ritual sufficed.

"Who's Benny Goodman?" I asked.

"A friend who plays the clarinet really well."

My father's right hand shook Benny Goodman's hand. When he worked as a fund-raiser for Jewish organizations, my father's right hand grasped the hands of presidents, astronauts, musicians, actors, and the philanthropically minded wealthy in America and abroad. His right hand opened doors for beautiful women and lit the cigars he smoked. It held the fistfuls of dirt he threw onto the coffins of his father, his sister, his mother, his brother, and his oldest nephew.

My father's right hand held the belt he used to punish my brothers; it held my own hand when I was a child. My father's left hand wore six different wedding rings; his right hand signed four separation agreements, over 2,340 alimony checks, and too many letters to attorneys. That same hand trembled as he inked his signature onto two do-not-resuscitate orders, one for his fifth and most beloved wife, another for his oldest son.

There on the critical care unit, padded, plastic mittens kept those hands restrained for the last eighteen hours of his life. His hands unable to handle.

My father appointed me his designated health-care surrogate, giving me the power to take him off life support, play God, end his dying. Here was a man who had indulged himself where women and gambling were concerned, a man who mitigated these compulsions with moderate spending and social alcohol consumption. I wondered how he felt having his hands—the instruments of his impulses—so limited.

I stood in front of my dying father. Dreading the possibility of having to invoke my authority as his surrogate and sign away what remained of his life, I still felt a certain satisfaction that he had chosen me to end things if he wound up suffering or lingering beyond repair. And there was, in the part of the brain that traps subtleties for later inspection, an echo of how peculiar it seemed that his hands, which had signed away other lives and thrown money on the casino table, were now bound while mine, innocent of these particular acts, felt weak and inadequate. I didn't like the *how* and *where* of his dying—if I could have arranged things, he would have been in his bedroom at home, propped up on freshly cased pillows, his favorite fleece blanket covering his disappearing body, Mary next to him holding his hand. I would have been sitting in his armchair, and, though I know it's selfish of me, Kyle would not have been there. No television, no cigarettes, no medications, no tubes. Just a tall glass of water by his bed. And instead of being half-present, he would have been lucid. Maybe he would say things he never dared to utter when he wasn't on the verge of dying: "I *did* once love your mother," or "I'm sorry I've been so afraid to talk about how I really felt about anything."

Instead, the whole scene was pierced with the kind of distractions that prevented me from feeling much of anything. First, the ride from the airport to the hospital, my brother Kyle—a chronically unemployed fifty-three-year-old man who lived with his eighty-nine-year-old mother (our dad's third wife) on the pretense of "taking care" of her—driving my father's car without a license (he hadn't renewed it for almost a decade) and narrowly missing at least three accidents in five minutes (the result of not having driven for so long and being under the influence of who-knew-what drugs). Mary rode shotgun and both of them talked at the same time, narrating the events of the day—"He was taken by ambulance to the hospital" and "He has pneumonia" and "A machine is keeping his blood pressure stable"—and as they spoke, all I could think was *how indelible a memory life is to the human heart.* Then the soap-opera walk down the hospital hallway, with the predictable push of the double doors to the CCU, the pneumatic *whoosh* ushering us into the austerity of critical care. When I stopped at the lavatory, panic, not grief, overwhelmed me: the sink, spattered with gray and yellow snot, and the wastebasket, overflowing with balled-up paper towels, had transformed this restroom into a claustrophobic refuge where people came not only to pee and shit but to cry and blow their noses into the sink before steeling themselves for the next episode with terminally ill family members or friends whose pee and shit and snot were siphoned out in tubes. And then the white-uniformed nurses who spoke in hushed tones at the counter where I signed the papers that would permit me to pull the plug if necessary. Finally, my father, shrunken into the bed behind a windowed wall with the curtain pulled back; any distinction to his death was eclipsed by the ubiquitous sharp smell of disinfectant and the softer, yet dirtier odor of near-death, the blipping and beeping of monitors, and the moans from a man in another room.

Trapped in the scene of his dying, my father was not attended by the comforts of home or the dignity of full consciousness, but restrained, his hands bubbled in plastic, his hair awry, his teeth on display.

What must be done . . . to honor the wishes of a man whose DNA humpbacked my pinkie toe, sculpted the bump in my nose, and stained dark semicircles under my eyes. To stop the breath of the father who denied he ever hurt my mother, who called her names even after she died and who didn't stop calling her names until thirty-eight years after their divorce, when I rose from the dinner table saying, "*Enough already, Dad.*" To pull the plug on the man who respected me alone of his two surviving biological children and trusted that I was smart or capable enough to get him out of this bind. But I could not release his hands from those mittens. No way I could orchestrate his fingers lacing around mine one last time.

There was nothing to do but wait. *I have become too good at this hanging around and waiting,* I thought. In Spanish, *esperamos* means "We are waiting," but change the context and it might mean "We are hoping." In French, *to wait* is *attendre,* whose root is familiar to English speakers as *attend,* a word that derives from the French word for *stretch.* In English, *wait* evolved from words that meant *to watch over* and, earlier, *to wake.* Waiting, then, is all of this—stretched hope, the attention of the awake, and watchfulness.

After our visit to the hospital, Mary, Kyle, and I returned to the apartment. Suspended in a deathwatch-induced insomnia, Kyle and I paced while Mary knitted and watched television.

"Your father wouldn't want to be that way," Mary said. "All those tubes." She set down her knitting to light a cigarette, her ninety-three-year-old eyes rheumy, her hands shaking.

"I have to wait at least twenty-four hours." I looked down at the tile floor as I said this, wondering how many times all of our feet had crossed this exact spot.

Waiting was my way out at that moment. The law mandates that three doctors must agree that a patient's life is no longer viable. The idea of a trio of physicians assembling on the critical care unit unnerved me. Besides, intensive *care* has always seemed the domain of nurses; doctors come and go, dealing with diagnoses and emergencies, looking at charts, making decisions, scrawling illegible signatures on papers. On the CCU, people are dying or close to it; some have died and been brought back; others have stopped living. According to the medical writer and surgeon Atul Gawande, some ninety thousand people linger in critical care across the U.S. on any given day. From the perspective of the patient's family and friends, the CCU offers not only the technology to maintain life, but a sense of exclusivity that, even if it cannot dignify death, at least can make it seem as if some special vigilance has been bestowed upon the dying. At these times, you want those guardian nurses rustling in their uniforms to speak softly when they must and attend to the bodies that were once animate; you don't want three doctors to hem and haw and examine charts and decide whether you should sign a piece of paper releasing a life. Your father's life.

"But how can you end it when he's able to look right at you, to know it's you and nod his head?" Kyle asked.

He had seen our father holding me tight with his eyes and probably resented it. Resentment was at the core of what was becoming just then a deep divide between my brother and me. Resentment that I had power of attorney and would be executor of the will, resentment that my father loved me most and made no attempt to hide his preference, resentment that I had made a life for myself when Kyle, an able-bodied man, was collecting disability in a state he no longer lived in and had been waiting four years for our father to die so he could get his hands on money he thought he had an inalienable right to inherit. Resentment that, when we were children, our father's belt came off for him, but never for me. My brother's resentment was and is more complicated than my assessment here; I know no one who has slipped through more cracks than he or deserved it less. I've come to suspect that Kyle's extraordinary musical talent, ability to memorize trivia, and facility with numbers probably derive from a form of Asperger's that escaped diagnosis.

This condition, aside from being unrecognized, has been exacerbated and transformed by decades of relentless self-medication with narcotics. His hostility toward me, regardless of its genesis, was unparalleled (no one else in the family ever treated me with such contempt), without compromise (the urgency of his bitterness poisoned the possibility of all of us exploring what was really happening), and unhelpful (try making a decision of any consequence when someone takes offense at your mere presence in the room). I wanted, just once, to attend to a familial death without the unraveling caused by the frenetic pace of my relations. But such respite was unavailable because, in my family, no one dies without trouble, and in this case, Kyle was the source.

"I don't envy you, Kimmie," Mary said. *There is no much not to envy,* I thought.

"How will you live with yourself?" my brother asked.

As my father died, his hands stopped living. *It's a drama of hands,* I mused, lighting one of the too many cigarettes I smoked that day.

Mary's old but still nimble fingers manipulated the knitting needles while Kyle poured juice to chase the fistful of painkillers (raided from Dad's bedside drawer) that he was popping into his mouth. Sealing us together in the apartment where my father had lived—among things he had touched (the blue and white clock in the kitchen, the telephone, the brass key on the door of the wood-and-marble bar)—was the humid August heat in south Florida. When you step out of a car or an apartment or an airport or a hospital, that heat is like an invisible wall, no cushioning whatsoever when you slam into it, and because air seems nonexistent, you can't even catch your breath.

My Father's Foot

Mary answered the phone at 2:00 AM, and I knew my father had spared me the burden of having to terminate his life.

We went to the hospital, traveling in a silence as dense as the heat. I was the first to see him. The mittens inflated around his hands stood out like something from a bad science-fiction movie. He wore only a hospital gown, those mittens, and tubes. His gown was parted and his genitals exposed. His skinny legs, which were once muscular and had propelled him through laps swum in the ocean, were twisted in the sheet and had become as useless as dried-out rubber bands. His penis—half the reason for his children's existence, the cause célèbre behind all the misery and heartbreak perpetrated over the course of more than seven decades—had retreated, was nothing more than one of many organs that had failed my father.

I covered his body and touched his foot, in spite of the long toenails, yellowed and ragged (*how connected,* I thought, *these digits of the hand to those of the foot; without use of the fingers, the toes fall into disrepair*). I touched the deep creases in the sole, which I imagined to be smoothing out as the seconds ticked by, moving my father backward from old age, through the robust years preceding his illness, past the headiness and virility of his manhood and the pliancy and curiosity of his adolescence and boyhood, and all the way to his smooth-footed infancy, before he could walk or talk, when he was as dependent on others as he was right before dying.

His foot moved. I knew rigor mortis was settling in, disturbing the stillness of his body, but I wanted to believe he was responding to my touch, that he wasn't beyond me or past the forty-five years we had shared as members of the same clan. Maybe he had not yet entirely vacated his body and was taking an imaginary walk, his feet transporting him across the beach, sand warm between his toes, or even down the hallway of his apartment, every step closer in his mind to some invisible destination—the water's edge, the front door, the elevator—every step nearer from my perspective in the CCU to his never moving again. I rubbed his feet and pulled the blanket over them.

I kissed his forehead. There would be no memorial service, no funeral, no interment. "What stays with you latest and deepest?" asks the speaker in Walt Whitman's "The Wound-Dresser." "Of curious panics, / and hard-fought engagements or sieges tremendous what deepest remains?" There was only this twitching foot and final good-bye that would remain, my lips on his broad forehead, a kiss that would remind me of all the nights he made this very same gesture when I was a child.

The last time you touch someone should be solemnified by silence. But as I withdrew my face from my father's forehead, I heard my brother, out in the hallway, asking someone for a pair of scissors. Whether he intended to or not, Kyle was interrupting the final moment of contact between my father and me. How typical his intrusion into our privacy, but even more so, how typical the collision between an act of grace and one that was ludicrous.

"Please," I asked a nurse. "Take out those tubes and close his mouth." I wanted Mary to have a proper good-bye.

Before the nurses attended to my father, Kyle waltzed into the room like a badly drawn cartoon of himself. His hair was dirty and matted. Stains on his shirt and pants ruined the effect of his having fussed over what to wear. He sidled up to the bed and assumed what he must have thought was a grief-stricken pose—head slightly hung, eyes pinched semishut to induce watering—so I could never say he looked or felt otherwise at that particular moment. He cut a lock of our father's white hair, which he pocketed along with the surgical scissors.

"Souvenirs," he said, all trace of the pseudo grief vanished.

My Father's Remains

My father wished to be cremated, and he had dotted every i and crossed every t to ensure that his last wishes would be followed. By the time he died, he had paid in full his "membership" in the Neptune Society, the funeral home that handled the cremation; he had made sure his will was up to date, and kept his executrix—me—regularly informed as to how he wanted things handled. On the death certificate ("You'll need it for *everything*," a paralegal told me), the sole pertinent fact is the exact cause of my father's death: his heart stopped. Nine decades of inhabiting his six-foot frame distilled into a filled-in blank, the words *cardiac arrest*—a term that always makes me think of the heart as some kind of criminal—scribbled in the EKG script of doctors that I'm able to decipher perhaps because my grandfather, uncle, and aunt were all physicians. Not even a complete sentence.

Months after my father was cremated, Kyle asked me to send him half of the ashes. Our relationship had deteriorated to the point where it was almost impossible for me to talk with him without having an anxiety attack. We left each other messages.

"Kim," he'd start, and I bristled as he pronounced that one syllable. "I'm going to Atlantic City this weekend and I want to leave some of Ab's ashes on the beach, so he'll be as near to the crap table as he can be. Let me know if you can make it. If not, send me my half of the ashes." Click.

My half of the ashes. "Asshole," I muttered as I dialed his number.

"Kyle," I started, wondering if he too angered at the sound of my voice and knowing he would never wonder if the sound of his annoyed me. "I can't make it next weekend. This is awfully short notice but I'll try to get you some of the ashes." Click.

"Kim, I told you last week. It is *not* short notice. Do I have to come to Pennsylvania to get my half of the ashes?" Click.

"Kyle, please remember that I work full-time, take my dog for chemo every other week, and otherwise am occupied with other responsibilities. I don't want to be asked to do things last minute." Click.

"Kim, all you have to do is call DHL—the ones with the red and orange shirts—or UPS—you know, the guys in brown—or FedEx, in that order of preference, and have them pick up the package. I'll pay for it." Click.

This conversation continued for two days.

I did not want to parcel out my father's ashes. I felt superstitious about dividing a man loved and hated by his two surviving children. Rationally, I knew my father's body was gone and it was not a *him* I was dividing, but *stuff* that was once him. But it's the kind of stuff that makes me irrational, and so I found myself contemplating whether my father's spirit resided in those ashes. What if, to be at peace, *all* your ashes must be in the possession of someone who loved you, not someone who only pretended to love you? Who watches when you handle that which remains?

Nevertheless, I had made a promise to Kyle. He needed to be appeased until I was discharged from the terrible task of executing my father's will. Terrible only because my brother behaved as if the stopper had been removed from his container of psyche, and unending toxicity—rage inherited from our father, anger about his own failures, grudge holding that could not be restrained—came pouring out of him onto me.

"I hate it when you yell at me," I told him once.

"Too bad," he said. "When I need to discharge my anger, I figure it's better to get it over with and move on."

"You don't understand, Kyle. It makes me shrivel up when you yell at me."

"Nothing I can do about it. Nothing I *want* to do about it."

I take the box of ashes into the bathroom, set it next to a small empty ziplock bag. But what to scoop them with? A spoon or a measuring cup seems wrong. I imagine myself scrubbing those utensils, unable to remove the residue of my father that only I would perceive, a stain invisible to others that would haunt me, until the implement wound up in the trash, which doesn't seem right, since I believe that whatever I use to complete this task should accompany the rest of the ashes when they are finally dispersed.

A scallop shell next to the sink catches my eye. I found this shell on a sand spit in northeastern Maine, and using it for the task at hand makes perfect sense. Shells were among the first digging tools. Perhaps graves were once dug with them. Maybe there were even separate middens where grave-digging shells were deposited. Legend has it that St. James journeyed across the sea cloistered in a scallop shell. And my father liked scallops. *Ashes to ashes, plastic bag to plastic bag, Coquilles St. Jacques to Coquilles St. Jacques*: here is my brief homage to a little bit of Torah, modern technology, and a Catholic myth insinuated in the French word for *scallop*. For a secular Jew who was a dedicated atheist, my father is getting a pretty spiritual send-off.

I open the bag and dip the shell into the ashes. I've handled remains before so I know what to expect in terms of texture—a grittiness, small sharp pieces, things that grind in the night. But I am unprepared for the slight tinge of pink—like finely ground pale rose quartz—I now see, and for the dust that rises from the bag as I disturb its contents. I should be praying, but I doubt anyone ever wrote words for the occasion of dividing a parent's remains. One scallop scoop and the dust rises and settles on the sink and wafts into my nostrils. I'm stunned into a state of complete inability to cry, not shock or numbness, more like time stopping. Second scallop scoop, each detail of this moment—my serious expression reflected in the wall-length mirror, a dried bubble on the ceramic soap dish, the dog standing in the doorway watching me, and the stuff I'm dishing out—inscribes itself so that I know nothing will stop me from one day telling this story. Third scallop scoop, I return to the here and now, the reality that my father's ashes are dusting my bathroom, and the pulse-quickening anger that shakes me as I recall that my brother had the nerve—no, the *gall*—to ask me to do this. Three scoops is enough. "Two scoops of raisins in every box," the ad for Raisin Bran suddenly intrudes in my mind. The absurdity is delicious to me, yet I don't want to be disrespectful at this particular juncture. I shake my head, as if that will make the jingle dissolve, close the plastic bag with its twist tie, and seal the ziplock bag, which I will pack in three padded envelopes before FedExing it all to my brother later that morning.

"You've helped him mourn," my therapist will tell me. "Even crazy people mourn."

I used to believe in cremation, mostly because it seemed like the most environmentally friendly option. And I still think it right to burn corpses riddled with incurable or virulent disease, to cleanse with fire. But ashes are so reductive, the packaging—plain metal tins and cardboard boxes—so mundane. It's the worst kind of smoke-and-mirrors trick, how you see someone dead and you're looking at their body, then you go away and the next thing you know that person is no longer contained in a body, but instead is a bag of dust and grit. If that's all it comes down to in the end, what's the point of pushing around the body and taking such pains to ensure its tone, beauty, or well-being? Maybe that is precisely the point, that there is no point, that we consume just so much space and time and oxygen in our physical incarnations, and once the heart stops and brain function ceases, the body, which shouldn't have mattered as much as it did in the first place, means nothing at all.

Ashes to ashes; ashes, ashes, we all fall down: the beginning, the end, the rapture and the descent, all wrapped up together. The burning of the body; the lives that are now but memories; the way the solid becomes particulate, more apt to vanish. All liquid is recycled; when it rains, it could be Nefertiti's bathwater falling on us, or the tears of a child lost in a snowstorm twenty years ago. Maybe all the ashes tossed into the air or sea or rivers, or those carried off funeral pyres by the wind, disperse and reappear too. All it takes is a scoop with a scallop shell to raise the dust of the dead and so breathe it in. I wonder if we respire particles that linger from the fires that burned the Great Library of Alexandria.

"In six months this will all be behind you," a man who is no longer my friend advised me after my father died. He had been a fleeting love interest. My dad's death was still new and raw and maybe that's why I held on to an idea that the possibility of some kind of romantic intrigue still lingered, even though whatever was between this man and me had ended and I knew it in that way you know things you can't admit you know. On the morning of the day he said this, I wore a scarf he had given me and a sweatshirt that once belonged to my father, and all too suddenly an awareness descended on me that I was wrapped in the clothing of two men who were dead in two different ways. It was brutal to absorb the notion that I was shrouded in articles each of them had once touched and worn, that my experience of both of them would live on only as memories, fading, compacting, and conflating as memories do. Just as that thought occurred, I felt the fissure spread across my chest and over my heart, the crack you cannot spackle or ever seal, the break in the heart that is such a cliché everyone knows there's a truth to it. I wanted to scream at this man for saying what he said, for being so emotionally vacant at that precise moment—no, I wanted to weep and be gathered in his arms—but he was too far away and weeping takes up too much time and I was on my lunch break and

I couldn't go back to work with swollen eyes and a hoarse voice. Faster to scream.

Screaming isn't my genre so I said—somewhat too blandly to be inconspicuous—"Uh huh." But when he uttered his pop-psych platitude, I wanted to tell him he had no clue and that wherever he picked up that glib phrase should be a place closed for eternity. I wanted to tell him that death is never behind you, and you can't put it anywhere; it's always around, lurking. Reminding. Playing tag. *You could inhale one of my relatives at any given moment.*

My Father's Teeth

Hours after our father died, my brother and I performed a cursory triage of Dad's personal belongings, or I should say, Kyle insisted that we agree right then and there who would take certain items. While Mary busied herself in the kitchen, he tore through the apartment, looking through bedroom dressers for pills and other spoils, stuffing things in his pocket, hoarding, telling me he would keep *all* the pipes, reminding me that he had counted *all* the cigars, and making sure I understood that despite my status as execu*trix* (disdainfully accenting the *tricks* I was certain to play on him), he, as the oldest surviving child, was in charge of everything. *Tricks,* I wanted to remind him, *are for kids.*

When he found my father's handgun, he unholstered it.

My heart pounded. "What if it's loaded, Kyle?"

He pointed it at my head. The look on his face said, *And so what if it is?*

"I never got to be here for any of the other deaths or moves," he said bitterly. "You got everything."

That day, Kyle stashed the smaller objects he had claimed in a cabinet, which I opened nine months later. Thrown inside with no apparent care were Dad's pipes, leather cigar cases, several pairs of dress socks, a heavy ashtray, empty pill vials, and, in a hastily twisted-closed Baggie, an assortment of things—mostly coins—that I knew had been pilfered from my father's bedside drawer. I picked up the Baggie, incredulous that Kyle was so needy he had to take a dead man's spare change. *Needy* might not be the right word; maybe my brother was trying to grab on to everything he could to feel as if our father had left him something special, something that said "I love you" in the ordinary way of change in your pocket. On closer examination, I saw that the bag also contained a couple of five-dollar casino chips, a small pearl-handled penknife, and a money clip, detritus scavenged from the bureau, or, looked at another way, evidence of my father's interests—casinos, tools, currency. But then I noticed something else in the collection my brother had assembled—one of those miniature plastic bags used for jewelry, and in it, six of my father's teeth.

I pocketed them. Mary could not know that those teeth were in the house, nor could she know that Kyle had tried to steal them, or that I was, as he'd see it, stealing them from him. They were, after all, encased in gold, which is probably why my father had saved them in the first place. Bullion in case of hard times down the road. The road to hell. A road, my father warned when we were children and misbehaved, "paved with good intentions."

My father lived to ninety and kept all but six of his teeth. By my midforties, I had lost only one of mine. Two of my brothers, on the other hand, had lost all of their teeth. Ron's had fallen out long ago, the result of heroin addiction. When he fell ill and came to live with me during the last year of his life, his false teeth had to be replaced because he had lost so much weight that the shape of his mouth had changed. All of Kyle's teeth were gone by the time he was forty-five. Dad paid for both his sons' dental restorations, a source of emotional agony for everyone involved since our father not only couldn't believe the prices, he never hesitated to remind everyone how astronomical the expense was, nor could he let anyone forget that *he* was paying for his children's neglect.

I know now why Kyle squirreled away those gold-filled teeth. The bag of coins was just a cover. He thought Mary or I would see the Baggie and neglect to carefully inspect it, thinking that if he was that desperate for some change, let it be. In my brother's perception, the teeth, I think, were proof that my father had lost a part of himself, that he was as vulnerable to decay as his two sons.

Ruins

With my intact teeth, oddly shaped pinkie toes, Ukrainian profile, and permanent shadows under the eyes, I resemble my father. Of his three biological children, I am the only one to make the throat-clicking noise he made; unlike my father, however, I don't simultaneously rattle the coins in my pocket, the tic that Kyle and I once joked was "having a frog in your throat and change in your pocket." Like my dad, I am good at getting reimbursed for accidental mishaps when traveling—able to finesse the broken hair dryer into an upgraded room or turn the two-hour delay on the runway into a voucher for a plane ticket. Like him, I am outraged by the injustice of the everyday: recordings in place of human operators (and the insidious menu options recited in automaton voices), the annual rise in the cost of postage, people who abandon or hurt animals, the complexity of stuff that should be simple, such as where your food comes from, tax returns, and health insurance. Like him, I adjust crooked pictures, and feel disturbed when things are aslant in any way small or large.

When I was growing up, it was not uncommon for my father to suddenly rise from the dinner table, interrupt conversation or the passing of a dish, and with one-track purpose furrowing his brow, straighten a painting on the opposite wall. When he sat down again, he resumed the conversation where he had left off, as if he had never moved.

Just the other day I came home from work and rehung a picture in my living room. It was too high, too far to the left. An etching by Piranesi that I inherited from my mother, which had hung on her living-room wall ever since I was a baby.

Fiddling with the picture, I looked at it closely, studied the people dressed in rags on a wide road under the shadow of a destroyed aqueduct, the whole scene rendered with Piranesi's architect sensitivity to scale and detail. The figures seem stalled—one stands looking out from an opening that might have been a door, another takes shelter near a stone wall, four are gathered around a wagon, and several are sitting on the ground.

Ruins make up one of the first visual ideas that entered my mind, a maternal legacy now on display where I live. The word *ruin* comes from the Latin *ruere,* to rush headlong, fall, collapse. An apt description for my parents' marriage, subsequent divorce, and seven years of custody suits; a perfect word to qualify Ron's and Ken's lives—one lost, the other destroyed beyond recognition.

Scraggly vegetation—nothing one might eat or even burn—grows on the stone arches. The place appears hot and parched, the occupants of the scene thirsty and hungry. Strange, though, for I am comforted by these ruins etched several centuries ago, reassured even by the implication that out of such poverty, life—or an affirmation of it—might remain. It does not surprise me that the ruin of this place occurred some time ago—flora with no value to those who live or linger there reclaims the architecture—and my lack of astonishment derives from a solemn, interior understanding that the ruin of my family was germinated at a time and in a place beyond anyone's memory.

teeth in the wind

*We forget that we are history. . . . We are not used to associating our
private lives with public events. Yet the histories of families cannot
be separated from the histories of nations. To divide them is part of
our denial.*

Susan Griffin, *A Chorus of Stones: The Private Life of War*

Cobscook Bay, Maine, 1995

"I'm frightened," said the little girl in the next room.

She was supposed to be sleeping, but a northerly wind rattled the
house, a cedar-shingled saltbox. The gusts whistled through the seams
between the roof and walls. Every so often a branch thumped against
my bedroom window.

Sophie, the child of a friend and a visitor in my house, called for
me again. I went to her room and stood in the doorway.

"I'm afraid," she whispered.

"Why?"

"Because there are ghosts in the wind," she said.

What if there *were* ghosts riding on the wind? Should I tell her I
wasn't sure? How much do you tell a four-year-old, especially one who
isn't your child?

"Ghosts can't hang on in a wind like this," I said. "They'll be torn
away. Anyway, I'm just in the other room. I'll leave the hall light on."

Sophie sat up. "But ghosts are *made* of wind," she said.

"No, honey, they're made of spirit. The wind won't hurt you."

Though I tried to speak with tenderness and authority, I doubted what I said. As if I needed proof of my own uncertainty, a series of recollections unfurled: the hurricane that splintered houses and scattered their parts so you could no longer tell where one dwelling began and the other ended; a freak May snowstorm that snapped old trees as if they were delicate bones; the thick smoke, hanging above the treetops, of distant forest fires stoked by the wind. I knew the wind causes great damage, but I wanted to believe just then in its potential for something like benevolence or solace. If it had been summer, I might have taken Sophie outside, picked a dandelion gone to seed, and watched with her as the breeze lifted its feathery spores. I wanted her to hear in the groaning bough outside my bedroom the strains of the first cello. Or understand—as Sir Francis Beaufort understood the poetry and violence of a near gale—that in a wind of thirty-nine to forty-six miles an hour the ocean "heaps up" and "streaks of foam spindrift" are formed.

I might have told her that for Boreas, the north wind, "It was hard . . . to breathe gently, and sighing was out of the question." Thomas Bulfinch, the nineteenth-century collector of myths, made this observation, and perhaps Sophie would have thought of Boreas as the kind of trickster who would sneak an extra cookie if no one was watching. Maybe then she could invent her own names for the wind, make up stories about it, and forget about the phantoms she imagined.

Instead I told her that ghosts are made of spirit and the wind wouldn't hurt her. How arrogant I was, how I wish I had sat on the edge of the bed and traced the outline of her forehead so she would fall asleep feeling safe. I might say I was unprepared for the responsibility of such a gesture. But as I tucked her in, I congratulated myself silently for my choice of words. It was as if I had passed a secret test on what grown-ups should say to children. I was proud to have invented safety out of thin air, and liked how literal it felt. It didn't occur to me that I was disguising my own apprehension. Nor did I see how I had crossed a threshold into complicity with every adult, including those of my own childhood, who left out not only information but also the truth of the stories that defined their lives—how they felt when trees snapped like bones, when homes crumbled, or when music issued from the bending trees. Leaving children like Sophie, who are afraid of wind or lightning, to uncover or imagine what had been omitted in the telling.

If there *were* ghosts, I pictured them as dark, bluish waves that shimmied through space, barely visible but for their long, sharp teeth. Such ghosts, I was certain, had ears that heard everything, including what was left unsaid. Perhaps these phantoms feed off our omissions. That would explain the ignoble, yellowed teeth.

Sophie called out just then.

"What is spirit?" she asked.

There are certain queries you cannot answer in the night when a northerly wind rattles the house, shakes the faith of a four-year-old, and compels the imagination to invent monsters. I knew I needed time to respond to such a complicated question. I hoped to run into Sophie when she was older. Maybe I could tell her then. Review the details, at least the ones I had encountered. That the Hebrew word *ruach* means—all at the same time—spirit, wind, and breath. That the tramontane, which heaves across the Mediterranean and then bangs into the Balearic Islands off the coast of Spain, has been used as a defense for acts of violence. That the word *tramontane* once identified the North Star. Such duplicity in heaven's breath. How could spirits not be involved? I pictured Sophie as a young woman, tall and lean, with long copper-colored hair. Maybe we'd run into one another at the grocery store, in the produce section.

"I'm sorry," I'd say as we reached for tomatoes, our hands barely touching, "that I didn't let you know about the danger of the teeth in the wind or the truth about ghosts or how spirits are different."

But Sophie was four, not twenty-four, and there was no future scenario I could imagine that would help me shape this present moment as something different. I should have known better, shouldn't have tried to fashion an illusion of safety, which is as hazardous as the danger it tries to hide. I had pretended that it wasn't possible for the wind to knock out a window. Or rip apart a section of roof. Down power lines and cause accidents, inconvenience, waste. By participating in the act of omission, I promoted a version of something that didn't exist.

I inherited an ability to suppress information from a long line of secret keepers, though this legacy was not always clear to me. Not long ago, I discovered that Kiev, where my paternal grandmother had us all believe she came from and lived, was neither her birthplace nor home. Why alter such basic information? What happened to my grandmother that she couldn't name for her family the town where she was born and raised, a place she finally left?

Somewhere in Czarist Russia, 1903–1911

Over a century ago, Fanya Weckstein was a girl of twelve living in the Pale of Settlement, a place whose name is derived from the Latin *palus,* an implement of boundary stabbed into the earth to demarcate a periphery. As a child, the phrase *Pale of Settlement* conjured for me a blurred, amorphous shape that faded in and out and described how things—snowflakes, perhaps, or ashes—fell into place. The Pale, like what is left out in the stories we tell, is vague and pointed, obscure and clear. Located in what is now western Ukraine, the Pale of Settlement served as a repository of the *unsettled* of czarist Russia, a locus for atrocities that in turn incited public and private silence and secrets: between 1903 and 1907, some fifty thousand Jews were murdered in the 284 pogroms carried out there; tens of thousands more were wounded and left homeless.

Speculating on my grandmother's omissions, I start by assembling facts. She was practically a teenager at the time of the 1903 pogrom in Kishinev, a town she would have traveled through on her way to visit cousins in Odessa. The violence at Kishinev in particular elicited international protest, so despite news traveling slowly at the time, one way or another Fanya Weckstein would have known of that particular pogrom.

Perhaps letters were sent that later disintegrated or were burned or lost. Maybe neighbors or other visitors came into her home and announced the news. I will never know if relatives were hurt or killed, or if my grandmother witnessed the violence firsthand by some unlucky coincidence. And how did she or her family react when they heard the news? Would their memory of the pogroms later conflate time, so that they forgot where the event started and the news of it began? Maybe they couldn't react visibly. Perhaps it kept them safe to make small talk, to pretend they didn't know what was happening. To discreetly make arrangements to send Fanya to America once her education was complete. And to never breathe a word.

My grandmother did not speak of growing up in the Pale, of Kishinev, or of the massacre at Odessa in 1905 where four hundred Jews and one hundred non-Jews were murdered. It was as if she denied ever having spent her childhood and adolescence in czarist Russia. I sense in this silence my grandmother's decision to sever herself from a body politic she adored but could not bear. Perhaps it is from her that I inherited this yearning to return, which might explain why, when she died, I wanted so badly to go back to her homeland. I was coming into my body—breasts budding, hips widening—as her physical familiarity and its comfort ceased to exist. But I knew that the ground on which she walked when she was my age still existed, and that I could, one day, walk on it too. There, I reasoned, I would somehow be reconnected with her. Of course I had no idea that my grandmother had removed her emotional and physical self from that *terra non firma*, first by the omission of where she came from, then by leaving the place she said she came from (as if it is possible to leave somewhere you never lived).

In February of 1911, Fanya Weckstein stepped onto the SS *Vaderland.* Her auburn hair fell to her thighs. When she landed at Ellis Island, she reported to a clerk, who in turn recorded the facts of her birthplace (Mintze), previous domicile (Mogilev-Podolsky), age (twenty), race (Hebrew), marital status (single), destination (Newark), and profession (student). This information is neatly penned into the ship's manifest.

I wonder if my grandmother decided to reinvent herself before she embarked or during the journey, if the short winter days and seemingly endless expanse of ocean—all that gray and cold—permitted her to design a different Fanya Weckstein, one who would never again speak of Kishinev, her home, her abandoned life, one who would disembark on the eastern seaboard of America free of regret. My grandmother never expressed a belief in God, but maybe she had made a deal with whatever divine presence she thought existed, as her family made plans to send her to America.

"I'll marry a stranger, answer your commandment to make children, and in exchange for your letting me off the hook of faith, I'll never disclose the hate and ugliness I've seen in the humans you created," she might have said.

In a family legend about my grandmother's journey to America, a young man falls in love with her during their ocean crossing. I look at the manifest for the SS *Vaderland,* at the names and ages and professions recorded there: perhaps it was the twenty-three-year-old tailor from Minsk who became enamored of Fanya Weckstein, the lovely woman who spoke Russian, Ukrainian, French, English, Yiddish, and Hebrew. Or maybe it was the youngest of the sixteen butchers also making that voyage whose heart was taken by this student from Mogilev-Podolsky. According to this legend, Fanya and the young man discussed literature. This is exactly the cue I need to create a visual of the story: my grandmother stands on the deck to take some air, the late winter sunlight twining in and out of her auburn hair, lightening her already pale green eyes, playing on her full lower lip. She talks about Chekhov, perhaps telling the young man that she feels like Masha in *Three Sisters,* dressed in black because she is "in mourning for my life." Or maybe they have a conversation about Pushkin and the duel that killed him. Fanya holds the rail of the deck to steady herself, and here the young man places his hand over hers. A daring gesture, full of longing. He tells her he wants to touch her hair. It's possible they never discussed literature, but science instead, and then I hear my grandmother talking about Marie Curie, a woman who left what had once been Poland and then became czarist Russia to live in France, and who had won the Nobel Prize in 1903, the same year as the pogrom at Kishinev. Between Fanya's intelligence and beauty, how could a young man *not* have fallen in love with her? It is said that he proposed to her, but she refused. Fanya Weckstein was on her way to America, a twenty-year-old picture bride who had left behind a Bolshevik lover and other mysteries to marry a doctor, an older man (who wore a stern expression behind round spectacles), who would become my grandfather. The story ends with the young man jumping overboard and drowning. And it also ends with my grandmother disembarking at Ellis Island and moving to Newark, New Jersey. When she married, she cut her hair.

Knowing that my grandmother fabricated the most ordinary detail of her life—where she was born and raised—makes me want to dismiss the legend. Yet I feel the story's pull on me, perhaps because it carries the kind of desire and loneliness I associate with the czarist Russia that backdrops every Chekhov drama. Maybe too in this fable another truth resides, one shaped by metaphor. Perhaps the part about the young man drowning is really about my grandmother's decision to never return to her home, to abandon any frivolous notions about love and construct a life built on omitted facts. Or maybe Fanya struck her bargain with God on the deck of the SS *Vaderland* and afterward created this story to disguise her own yearning.

Cobscook Bay, Maine, 1995

Sophie finally fell asleep. The slow in and out of her breathing was small and light against the hiss-and-whistle haphazardness of the wind and the punctuating thump of the branch against the window. The ticking of the clock, which usually disturbed my ear, soothed me with its regularity.

Sophie's unanswered question about spirit lingered. Why would I imagine bluish ghosts biting into the wind with incisors borrowed from a creature out of a horror film? Wind and storms remind me that when trees topple and homes fall apart, I should live in the present, that any grasp on the world is tenuous, including the hold of deep tree roots and the foundations of houses. At thirty-five, I had some ideas about spirit that I kept mostly to myself, but I didn't believe in ghosts. At least I had never seen any. I couldn't figure out why I kept seeing those teeth. What danger rode on the wind? Windows and roofs are replaceable. Accidents happen. Power goes out. These are ordinary events, mostly nuisances, sometimes serious or even heartbreaking. But still ordinary in the sense that they occur with habitual frequency and are expected to a degree, even when they're unexpected.

It would take me years to articulate the vague sense I had then of history taking place as a series of everyday transactions—including the exchange of omissions—between ordinary folks. It hadn't occurred to me yet that we've forgotten, as Susan Griffin writes, that "we are history," that our private denials might bolster or mirror collective ones. But on that night in 1995, even if I couldn't verbalize what I was thinking, I was preoccupied with figuring out if I had ever accidentally stood on the threshold of some kind of silence. Not one of my own, but the kind that informs history or alters how the everyday business of life is conducted. And what if I *had* stood on some edge—did my presence there complicate or unscramble the silence? The branch outside my window thumped, and a muscle constricted in the back of my neck. As I placed my hands behind my head and pressed my fingers into the tightness, a memory surfaced that I hadn't considered for some years.

Toulouse, May 1986

Nap on the grass in the park, I printed in a notebook on May 2, 1986, several hours before the news of the explosion at the Chernobyl nuclear plant was first released in France, where I lived when I was in my midtwenties. I was in the city of Toulouse visiting my friends Eric and Pierre. I watched ducklings on a pond before easing my back onto the grass and closing my eyes.

I had never been in this city before. Its unfamiliarity, dipped in the vivid colors of blossom and new life, anchored for me the interval between *not knowing* and *knowing* about the world's worst nuclear disaster. As the ducklings glided on the pond, Soviet authorities questioned operators from the V. I. Lenin Atomic Energy Station; some of these men would be arrested, though the meltdown occurred because of design flaws, not operator errors. I napped in the first sun of that spring, as ignorant of them as they were of me. They were irradiated, interrogated, and in a state of shock, their lives out of focus. I watched ducklings with wobbly legs and untried wings, each feather outlined with an acuity that preserved a fragile but lucid "moment of being," as Virginia Woolf called it, a sensation that is possible when you feel completely safe, or on the edge of panic or immersed in madness.

After my nap, I returned to Eric and Pierre's apartment and helped prepare dinner. A gentle breeze billowed the floor-length white curtains. The news about Chernobyl came over the radio. Outside, a tree moved in the wind.

Eric turned off the radio after the broadcast.

"We could die from this," Pierre said.

And then we stopped talking. We ate in silence, except for the sound of silverware against the plates and the whisper of breeze that riffled the curtains. We left the dishes in the sink. Eric put a record on the turntable and the three of us danced, bringing our bodies as close as possible to each other.

What did we leave out? Thinking back to the moment of that radio broadcast, I don't recall my hands shaking, or tears, or even a hint of headache behind my eyes. But I feel the sudden desire I had to be physically close to Eric and Pierre, to know that I was flesh and that my skin could register friction. And I sensed too a similar longing in these two young men, beyond the electrochemical impulse of desire, a yearning for intimacy as we censored our terror that the world as we knew it had irrevocably changed.

I find it peculiar that I only recorded my nap in that notebook. I did not write one comment about the catastrophe at Chernobyl. In the days following the news of the explosion, however, I took pains to catalog my meandering in Toulouse. I noted where I went: to a quarry and a bar. And what I did: left the quarry and the bar, stayed up all night, and walked around in the bareness of 5:00 AM with nothing but the aroma of baking bread to comfort me. I never wrote about the ducklings, nor did I observe how I felt. Maybe I didn't need to. Later I would be able to summon, simply by looking at photographs of Eric and Pierre, the serenity by the pond and the shakiness afterward when we learned about Chernobyl. Now I might describe my fear as resembling the terror of all language becoming incomprehensible in a single instant. Like knowing there are teeth in the wind, or seeing malevolent ghosts in the gusts of a northeaster. Like a nuclear reactor exploding while ducklings line up one by one to follow their mother and father into a pond and float away on the water's uninterrupted surface.

I was only twenty-six, and didn't know then that memory has a tendency to compress time. Perhaps this temporal conflation occurs because when we are not yet all grown up but think we are, the present is simply an obstacle to the future. For years I believed that the broadcast *about* the Chernobyl disaster and the actual event were separated by a few hours. I know now that there was no reliable or accurate news about the explosion until days—and in some places weeks—later. It would take more than a decade for me to understand that this particular silence was the kind that shape-shifted. It was a silence that began as misinformation, such as the International Atomic Energy Agency's assessment that the risk of cancer as a result of the disaster would be "undetectable." Rapidly it mutated into censored facts—the tens of thousands of cesium-contaminated reindeer slaughtered in Lapland, and the devastation that particular government action had on the indigenous Sami, not to mention levels of cesium-137 detected more than fifteen years later in British sheep and American milk. The public record became a forum for debate—between the international nuclear establishment, government agencies, grassroots organizations of people with radiation-related cancer, and environmentalists—about how dangerous the accident was. Eventually the misinformation and censorship eroded into communal amnesia and muteness.

Chernobyl, April 26, 1986

At a little past one in the morning on April 26, 1986, several operators at the V. I. Lenin Atomic Energy Station in the Ukrainian town of Chernobyl conducted a test to see how long the generators of reactor number four would run without power. If I could produce a photograph of that moment, it would show one of those operators just prior to the test. He shuts his eyes for an instant to imagine Halley's Comet, a mass of ice and stone with a vaporous tail, moving through the constellation of the wolf, as it traveled that day in 1986. As close to the earth as it could come without touching.

Why shouldn't I imagine him contemplating the heavens? The word *Chernobyl* is the Russian name for the star Wormwood, and refers to a prophecy of poisoned rivers and doom in the book of Revelation. "And there fell a great star from heaven," it is written, "burning as it were a lamp."

The operators disabled safety systems so as not to interfere with the test. Their hands hovered over the controls, and their fingers trembled slightly, perhaps, as they called out checklisted protocols and threw switches. By 1:23 AM, things weren't right, and maybe one of the men wiped his brow as another pushed the button to engage the automatic protection system. Within three seconds, the operators saw the gauges in the control room registering that the reactor's core had surged to one hundred times the normal level. At exactly 1:26 AM, the explosion occurred, blowing off the two-thousand-metric-ton metal plate that had sealed reactor number four. Shock waves as strong as a mild earthquake shook the plant, whose core would melt down by the time this accident completed its cycle. A decade would pass before these and other pieces of information were released, assembled, interpreted, understood.

"It seemed as if the world was coming to an end. . . . It was a nuclear hell," wrote the man who oversaw the shift at Chernobyl that night.

Toulouse, May 1986

A week after the explosion, but only two days after hearing the news about it, I boarded a train in Toulouse and looked out the window. On the platform, folks waved and kissed good-bye, looked for the right car, shifted bags from one arm to the other, scolded children for running, and generally went about the everyday business of getting themselves or someone they knew onto a train. It all seemed too normal, so I checked my ticket to make sure I was on the correct train, in the right seat, headed to the proper destination. I sensed a weight and measure to things that I had not experienced before the news of Chernobyl, as if the acuity I felt watching the ducks at the park had spread to my other senses. The sound of the wind had a heft that I hadn't noticed before. Daylight emitted an odor of metal and skin, and my body seemed light, as if it were suspended in time. In the slight give to the leather seat, I felt the weight, the distance, and the closeness of other lives.

A man in gray wool trousers and a tweed jacket entered the compartment and sat across from me. If either of us had had longer legs, or if there had been less space between the seats, our knees would have touched. The proximity amazed me since we're taught to maintain boundaries in public, especially with strangers. And also, I was pre-occupied by the things that fill time and space. Who designed those seats in a train; what equation was used to calculate the distance sepa-rating our knees? How are the borders determined between public and private?

As the train pulled out of the station, the man unfolded his news-paper. I turned away from the newsprint suspended between his hands and watched the city give way to an expanse of fields blurred together with the tender May-greened trees and the feverish yellow, purple, and bright pink of spring flowers. This might be the last time I would ever see this landscape dressed in such splendor. Nature, at least, omits nothing; it was abundant even at the moment I was start-ing to think of as the beginning of the end.

The man stopped reading his paper, ran a hand through his thin gray hair, and started a conversation. Where are you from, where are you going, you speak French with almost no accent, that sort of thing. I resisted the urge (and I did not yet know where this impulse came from) to make up a story about my origins, tell him I was Canadian, for example. I could have said anything, I realized, and how would he have known what was true and what wasn't? The truth was that I didn't feel as if I was *from* anywhere—I was on my way to an empty apartment that I would leave in several months for another empty apartment, and the place I thought of as my family's homeland had just been obliterated by a nuclear accident. Furthermore, my ability to speak French commenced with the unpleasant requirement of sit-ting in Miss Brown's elementary-school classroom for too many years, repeating the same words to the point of numb perfection, terrified she'd whack my fingers with her yardstick if I made a mistake. Not in the mood to exchange the pleasantries that prevent us from getting too close, I glanced instead at the newspaper he had folded and set on the seat beside him.

The man gestured to the headline above the fold. "If France can deny American military planes access to French airspace," he declared, "perhaps we should refuse passage to the nuclear cloud from Chernobyl."

I responded with silence. The statement seemed out of place and irritating, too glib, too great a dose of denial's bad taste. But instead of saying any of that, I nodded and looked away. We were strangers on a train and our knees almost touched. I wanted to close my eyes and feign sleep, but I was too absorbed by how everything outside—the clusters of stone houses, the mustard fields alternating with bright green pastures—seemed to move as I sat still, a perennial sensation that I experience on trains. The weight of my dispassion for the man spread through my chest as a tired heartburn that no amount of antacid would neutralize. The tiny space between our legs became a distance that expanded until it was measureless. Even if I had shut my eyes, I could not shut him out, nor would I forget the unbuttoned tweed jacket, his slight paunch, the wrinkles in his shirt.

Thinking I might stop all potential conversation, establish a boundary between us, I asked if I might read his newspaper. He nodded, picked up the paper, and as he handed it to me, I saw his wedding band. A simple ring, the gold dulled and softened with years, it had a smooth, solid look, as if it were part of his hand, a thing he had never removed. I wanted to ask him where his wife was, if he was rushing home to hold her or assure her that Chernobyl could not touch them, if he really believed that was true, or if he was headed into her arms and comfort, or if he planned on buying her flowers. *Roses*, I wanted to say, *buy her three dozen roses of every color, even if you cannot afford them*. Instead I thanked him, opened the paper, and from behind it I looked out the window.

When I arrived home, I turned on the radio and listened to the advisories, the hushed debates about what levels of fallout were considered safe, and the recommendations to thoroughly wash produce. I watched myself and others do as we were told without raising our

voices too often or too loudly in question or protest, as though radiation were as superficial as dirt. Rinse it away and watch it spiral down
the drain.

Eventually, other news replaced the little we were told about
Chernobyl. Occasionally I slipped and forgot to wash the vegetables.
After a month or so I no longer talked about the explosion or the contaminated cloud that drifted west or north, but I wondered how we
might adapt to a life of endless chain reaction. Sometimes in mirrors,
I glimpsed myself as if I had x-ray vision. I could not name what I saw
in my reflection, but I sensed it as a hollow despair, the kind that awak-
ens you from a dream of losing all your teeth.

Cobscook Bay, Maine, 1995

In the deep silence of 2:00 AM that comes after a storm subsides, the
house settled, the cat shifted on a chair, the dog stretched, and Sophie
turned on her pillow. I heard in all those small noises not emptiness
or things that had been left unsaid, but the slumber of normalcy. The
wind had passed, but what had it left behind, and what had it carried
away? I rubbed my neck and turned out the light.

In the darkness, I contemplated that man on the train. Maybe he
had been away from his wife because their marriage was failing. It's
possible that his wedding ring was worn because he rubbed it absently
or nervously, like a worry bead. Maybe he was trying to flirt with me
and I had missed that, or perhaps he was simply on his way to visit
someone for the weekend—a family member, a mistress, a child who
had grown up and moved away. I should have asked him why he had
made that silly statement about government and radioactive clouds.
Or let him know, at least, that I was feeling quite doomed that day,
not up for that brand of sarcasm. What if I had shifted in my seat and
our knees had touched, or what if I had reached across the space between us and taken his hands and told him I was scared, not only of
radioactive clouds, but of empty homes and emptier pronouncements,
and of loneliness?

In May of 1986 I didn't know that 190 tons of radioactive uranium and graphite had hitched a ride on the wind directly over my home in eastern France. One hundred and ninety tons. I get stuck there every time because I'm unable to visualize such a weight, even if I imagine (which I can't) 190 one-ton trucks lined up in a row. After my visit with Eric and Pierre, and there in the train with a stranger, I was only thinking about particles, how the smallest things separate us, and that even when we hold hands or kiss or otherwise connect, there is still atomic matter between one person's skin and another's. Perhaps that particulate boundary is necessary when we live in a world where, on trains, the knees of two strangers almost touch. But silence may fill those spaces, and, as my grandmother probably knew when she was seized by the heart attack that claimed her life, what we do not say lingers, changes form, is transmitted.

In 1986, Lyubov Sirota—a young mother who lived in Pripyat, a satellite city three kilometers from the Chernobyl nuclear plant—had not yet written her poetry about the disaster. Mikhail Byckau—a physicist at the Nuclear Energy Institute of the Belarusian Academy of Sciences in Minsk—had not yet recorded his testimony about Chernobyl. But in 1995, as the wind pushed against my bedroom window and a little girl slept in my cedar-shingled house in Maine, I imagined what it would be like if they had met, two strangers whose lives were connected by the same event:

> Lyubov and Mikhail sit on the edge of a crater where reactor number four, the one that exploded, used to be. They swing their legs in the dark void of the hole. Sometimes their knees touch.
>
> "How can this be?" Mikhail asks. "The reactor was never removed."
>
> Lyubov is a petite woman. All her shiny blonde hair has fallen out. She keeps touching her head, as if to confirm its baldness.

"It was a warm and clear night, and I couldn't sleep," she says. "I stepped out onto our balcony and smelled the apple and cherry blossoms. Then I saw a giant flash of light, as if a star had burst through the sky."

Mikhail nods. He takes her hands, closes his eyes. Many of his teeth are gone. Those that remain are yellow or chipped or loose. Lyubov raises her hand to feel her own teeth, and her face relaxes when she finds them intact. Still, she wishes she had a mirror to check.

"I went to work and switched on the apparatus," he says. "The instruments we used to monitor radiation—the gamma spectrometer, the dosimeters—they were all hot. We thought there had been an accident there in Minsk, on the premises of the institute."

"Spectrometer—does it detect ghosts?" Lyubov asks. "Or does it have something to do with spectrum? Does it pick up apparitions, things that are invisible? What does a spectrometer look like, how does it work?"

Mikhail doesn't answer her.

Lyubov raises her eyes to the night sky. "Saturday, April 26, 1986, was a sunny day. Women in loose, light dresses and bareheaded men walked in the streets of Pripyat," she says. "Children were eating ice cream, infants sleeping in strollers. When I saw the two men approaching in their shiny protective clothing—the gloves, hoods, and military-issue respirators— I knew something was wrong."

Mikhail sighs. The knees of his trousers are threadbare. His hair is white.

Lyubov reaches her thin arms toward the sky. Bruises cover the insides of those pale arms. "In Pripyat, *nobody* knew anything," she says.

Mikhail removes his wire-rim glasses and throws them into the crater. "The frames were bent, and besides, I can barely see anymore," he tells Lyubov. They laugh.

"Frantically, we telephoned family and friends, repeated the safety measures we knew by heart, but by noon the phone lines were cut off," he says. "When I went home from work, it was all I could do to keep from screaming—there were children playing in the radioactive sand and eating ices. In our street I went up to a vendor and told her to stop selling sausages, that radioactive rain was falling. She accused me of being a drunkard and pushed me away. She said if there had been an accident, she would have heard about it on radio or TV."

"Here," Lyubov says, turning in a slow circle and throwing her arms in a wide embrace to the barren landscape around the crater, "chokecherries came out with white flowers like gamma fluorescence. Tomatoes ripened too early: someone just ate one—the ambulance had to be called in a rush. We have slipped up."

My hair was damp, the sheets in disarray when I awoke several hours later. A slant of sunlight through my bedroom window caught in its beam the particles of dust rising from the carpet. Sophie was still asleep. I pulled on jeans and a heavy sweater and went outside for some air. Two crows cawed back and forth. A squirrel peeked out from the underbrush of the woods surrounding the house. Chickadees twittered in the spruce. Here and there the storm had pruned the trees, scattering branches, limbs, and twigs at random. The wind had undressed the maples and birches of their foliage. The bay, scrubbed the previous night by whitecaps and swells, was placid.

Kiev, 1991

Five years after the disaster at Chernobyl, I traveled to Kiev, in spite of my fear of contamination. I had imagined that the entire area around the city would have been declared a forbidden zone if it were truly unsafe to travel there. Besides, I thought as I purchased my tickets, the fallout had already dusted my produce. I vowed to buy bottled water and avoid root vegetables (*what a fool,* I thought later, staring into bowls ladled full of potatoes, carrots, beets). I compared my abstract fear of contamination with the concrete reality of radiation burn victims or displaced families (environmental refugees, they are called), and scolded myself for overreacting. It was, I finally decided, more important to be the first in our family to touch the ground of ancestors and walk among their spirits. I had nurtured a dream of making this voyage for over twenty years.

I didn't know when I arrived in Kiev that my grandmother had never lived there. I had invested that city with all the properties of a link back to her, and attached to it a tangle of nostalgia, that urge to return. I would find there, I was certain, some vestige of my grandmother as a young girl and answers to questions I never asked her when she was an older woman. Such as where she took her first steps, or if she sat on the riverbank and contemplated her love for a man who would marry her best friend, or how she felt when she was forced to leave her home because she was a Jew.

No one had ever told me her story. And I didn't realize that no one *knew* her story because she had kept it so well hidden. After hearing the news about the explosion at Chernobyl, one of my first thoughts was that I would never make this trip, one I had imagined since I was eleven. When I listened to the radio newscaster in Toulouse— the voice that left out the details later divulged—the girlhood of my grandmother seemed locked behind a door that was slammed shut in the early morning hours of April 26, 1986. Any chance I had of looking at the world I thought my grandmother saw when she came of age seemed incinerated.

The world I thought she saw. I arrived in Kiev on a bus, beheld the apple blossoms, and felt certain that Fanya Weckstein had rested her eyes on those same trees. Walking the streets in the Jewish quarter, and unaware that she would have required a special residency permit to live in Kiev, I claimed to sense my grandmother through my feet, as if a mystical osmosis reconnected us. I infused buildings and scenery with her gaze, placed her on the grand boulevards and on a bridge that crossed the Dnieper River.

How naive. To construct a memory of someone else's past is, perhaps, one of nostalgia's greatest lures—to return to a place that someone else had come from and lived in and left. Then again, what did I have to work with? Photographs with inscriptions on the back, one family legend, and finally, my own attachment to my grandmother, to the warmth of her old-woman body, her fleshy arms and white hair, her willingness to play cards with me when she spent the night. The memory of her imploring me to "Go fish, Kimche, go fish." I wanted to know this grandmother as Fanya Weckstein, a young woman not yet plucked out of the life she knew as a girl, wanted to contextualize her in a place where she was safe in spite of a history that said otherwise.

Only one synagogue is active in Kiev. The bus driver announced, loud enough for everyone to hear, that he wasn't sure where it was located. But with a silent aside—the slightest movement of his eyes to the left, the quickest jerk of his head—he revealed that a building across the street, whose top peeked out over a high wall, was *that* synagogue.

White trim accentuated this place of prayer and gathering, the outside walls painted a red between burgundy and crimson. Nothing on the exterior wall or gate indicated the practice of the faithful within. I was astonished by the use of color, not only in Ukraine, but everywhere in the Soviet Union. The contrast between the older buildings—painted light ocher, periwinkle, salmon—and the impersonal, flat gray concrete of newer structures reminded me constantly of my own oscillation between two geographies. In Kiev, I was somewhere very far from home. On the other hand, I believed that I *was* home.

What I didn't know was that I was *not* home, and when I made that discovery fifteen years later, I would see not only the myth I had created of Kiev but also the illusion of returning to a place from which I had never departed. I would realize how invested I had been in a false homecoming, and wonder how I might ever forge of this memory a truth that belonged to me.

I entered the courtyard of the synagogue. Maybe my mouth was open; definitely my eyes were wide and wet. As I watched children playing, an old man placed his hand lightly on my shoulder. I turned to face him.

He was a grandfather, and the first witness to Chernobyl whom I met. Equipped only with the desire to communicate, neither of us had the tool of fluency in the other's language. I watched his hands—fingers swollen with years of physical labor, creased palms—and how they spoke. He punctuated his gestures with Russian, some broken English, but mostly with Yiddish. It was his hands, though, that described the expanses of skin peeling off the bodies burned by the explosion at Chernobyl.

As I traveled around Kiev, people with whom I had no relation claimed my attention. My grandmother, I sensed, might have been in this city, but she had left and there must have been a reason for her never returning, not even once. I could not find any trace of her, not in the synagogue where she would not have prayed, nor in the Soviet art that decorated the walls of concrete housing projects that had sprung up in the suburbs. The people I met in Kiev grappled with the immediate effects of Chernobyl, not metaphorical teeth snapping in the wind; they lived there in the long half-lives of radionuclides from which they could not escape. Suddenly, I found myself collecting their stories.

I visited with a journalist who told me that in May of 1986, Ukrainian radio broadcasts recommended taking showers after outdoor excursions. He walked his Afghan hound in the park, wiped off his shoes with a wet rag by the door when he came home, and showered in his clothes with the dog. He never let on if he cried through any of this. Or what he did with the towels after those showers. Or if the dog lived.

Another journalist, a French woman of Ukrainian descent, described how leaking reactors at Chernobyl were unsuccessfully contained, which resulted in additional radiation being spewed into the atmosphere. This information was never released to the public, she said, almost in a whisper. The woman told me she believed there was no such thing as "off the record," and so she had dedicated herself to pursuing and telling the truth.

"But no one wants to listen," she said. Except certain doctors in Paris, who raised their eyebrows and lowered their glasses when the journalist explained that she traveled frequently to the Kiev area. "Then they want to run all kinds of test *on me.*"

I befriended a Ukrainian university student. One day, he confided, he would describe what happened, what it was like when the illusion of safety was shattered by Chernobyl.

"But first I must write my novel about how love fails." He said he recognized the connection between love's failure and the lost control of a nuclear reactor, but he refused to make the link in his writing. "I get depressed. I'd end my life if I couldn't hold on to some kind of hope," he explained.

I listened to a woman from Kiev tell me life was simply too short to worry. "I'll sit on the beaches of the Dnieper in the summer, as young people have always done," she said, "even though I know those sands swell with radioactivity." I looked at the riverbank as she spoke and could make out my grandmother sitting there at the turn of the twentieth century.

The trees shade her. Icy gray speckles lace her eyes of pale green, a color she would bequeath to my father. She wears a hat, sits on a blanket, and dares to remove her shoes and wiggle her stockinged toes in the sand. Perhaps she's thinking of the man who has addressed her as *comrade* and written poetic inscriptions on the backs of old photographs. He's engaged to her best friend and my grandmother is about to abandon this intrigue and leave for America. She contemplates the wind moving in the apple trees. A young woman on the threshold of departure, ready to reinvent herself.

I blinked and my grandmother disappeared.

Cobscook Bay, Maine, 1995

In the polished morning after the storm, I turned my thoughts to the mundane acts of feeding the dog and cat, emptying the trash, making beds. Sophie would awaken soon, and perhaps we would walk in the woods or along the water's edge. I hoped she had forgotten her questions about ghosts and spirits, that I would be let off the hook of not being able to respond.

Perhaps we participate in acts of omission to shape memory into something manageable and safe. Who has the room inside their psyche to remember everything, carry the weight of how things felt, and still get out of bed each morning? It's easier to operate within the facts, to describe our lives as a series of events instead of disclosing at every turn the experiences of the body and the mind. Simpler to say that a hurricane destroyed a house than to describe your accelerated heartbeat or the thousand-yard stare you mastered when you saw your home splintered. Less complicated to talk about the old trees falling with muffled thuds in the unexpected May snow than to admit you startled or cried each time one snapped. More concrete—and perhaps more polite—to play a Yo-Yo Ma CD than to explain how your chest expands and contracts when you hear trees orchestrating their own music.

Maybe we create gaps in memory for the same reason that we forget physical pain. When I fail at recalling any kind of discomfort I've felt—from migraines to paper cuts—I marvel at our human design. Of headaches, I'm able to recount the details—the too-bright sunshine, or the odor of plant fertilizer that exacerbated my nausea—environmental conditions that seemed unbearable on the days I lay in bed, the upper right part of my forehead pulsing so hard I thought I needed to go to the emergency room. But the throbbing ache above my eyebrow is lost to me—I know it was once there, but I cannot retrieve that physical memory.

I'm preoccupied with how the practice of secret keeping begins, with putting my finger on the origin of behavior as easily as I might touch a map to locate a town or a river. Perhaps pinpointing these intersections—of time and geography, the movement of ordinary lives along those continua—will help reshape a memory fractured by omissions. But that's not all. Maybe understanding the genesis of omission in my family is one way to undo the silences such a habit engenders. And I suspect that knowing where the gaps are—identifying what has been left out—contextualizes the business of remembering. I'm not sure what I mean by this, only that without context, both memories and omissions lose their meaning.

I want to finish telling my grandmother's story, but I can no longer separate it from Chernobyl. Like the people evacuated from the contaminated zones, Fanya Weckstein was a refugee, though we use the word *immigrant* as a way of ignoring the causes of exile. There are moments when I imagine her as having the gift of prescience, of knowing that communism would fail the Jews of the Pale, or that a nuclear disaster would occur in Ukraine, that she should leave and build another life somewhere else simply because she had survived extermination on the same soil. In more skeptical instances, I realize that I think such things in order to justify the coincidence of occurrences in Ukraine that generate refugees and exiles and shifting borders from century to century with alarming frequency.

Sometimes I believe that I really did see my grandmother there on the banks of the Dnieper River, her shoeless toes sifting the white sand. Maybe she's still sitting there, dreaming a different life for herself, a life in which she keeps her hair long and raises the children of another man in a country where she doesn't have to hide where she was born or came of age.

Sophie came downstairs.

"The ghosts are gone," she said.

On the Beaufort scale, the wind now registered as a two, otherwise described as caressing the face, rustling leaves, and moving ordinary vanes. I wondered how Sir Francis Beaufort might have answered Sophie's question about what makes or resides in the wind.

"Yes," I lied. "They're gone."

Quoted material in the passage on pages 90–92 has been adapted, in part, from the following sources: 1. Mikhail Byckau, "Chernobyl: Once and Future Shock, A Liquidator's Story," trans. Vera Rich, Index on Censorship, Jan. 1996, and 2. Lyubov Sirota, "At the Crossing," trans. Leonid Levin and Elisavetta Ritchie, Chernobyl Poems by Lyubov Sirota, ed. Paul Brians, 14 Dec. 2005 http://www.wsu.edu/~brians/chernobyl_poems/chernobyl_poems.html.

wings over moscow

These days one must fly—but where to?
without wings, without an airplane, fly—without a doubt:
the footsteps have passed on, to no avail;
they didn't move the feet of the traveler along.

Pablo Neruda, XCVII, *100 Love Sonnets*

Preparing to Fly at Night

Three months before the fall of the Soviet Union in May of 1991, I watch hooded crows circle above the housing projects outside of Moscow. In the predawn sky, the pearl gray bodies of the birds seem like muffled lights. I've been traveling with Irina, a woman I know from Paris, both of us descended from Russian Jewry. We are the first in our families to return to this place we think of as a homeland, though for her father and my grandparents, Russia was a point of departure, a place they left without looking back. We've come here to fulfill some kind of ancestral errand in an attempt to complete a journey started by someone else, in search of something we never lost, but which we feel responsible for finding. Of course, no one has told us exactly what we're supposed to find, or where to look, but for Irina and me the act of return—to the place where that something was lost—seems like the first step. It would be easier to be a salmon, I think, the map of birthplace inscribed in body and brain, the homecoming a genetic necessity instead of some vague notion handed down by relatives who never really discussed the reasons for their leave-taking.

Irina wears her dark hair short, a style that accentuates her profile. Her eyes are dark too. We've been thrown together by a mutual association, a man who said to me, "Oh, you must meet Irina," and to her, "Oh, you must meet Kim." And so we've met and discovered in one another what our friend saw: a passion for the visual, which Irina records in photographs and I preserve with words, a preoccupation with the pasts of our respective families, and the urge to go back to a motherland we've romanticized, to look for something we think has been lost.

We haven't found it. Furthermore, tensions exacerbated by sharing close quarters, not sleeping enough, and drinking too much have escalated to the point where Irina and I have lost our ability to talk to one another about anything more than our basic impressions of where we are or how to get from one place to the next. "It's a bit chilly today," one of us says so politely I feel nauseous. "Don't you think we ought to take a left onto this avenue?" the other asks as we emerge from a subway station.

Now we're standing here at dawn, involved in a discussion about the last leg of this journey, the trip to the airport. I look to the sky, as if the promise of sunrise in Moscow could change anything. As if morning might reveal that our suitcases—packed with books and caviar and lacquered boxes—are filled not with ordinary tourist trappings, but with proof of a homecoming we were obliged to make when we became the granddaughters of immigrants. Of course such substantiation cannot be located in stores where the clerks remove books from locked glass cases, or purchased on the street where black marketeers open long overcoats to display the wares pinned and pocketed inside (lacquer jewelry, jars of sturgeon roe, Soviet watches). That evidence is as vague and unreliable as our reasons for being in Moscow. I'm beginning to suspect that what we've been looking for is merely a feeling, a taste, a smell—some sensory confirmation that Russia holds our origins.

The gifts we've bought and the rolls of film in our bags make for the only tangible evidence of our having been here. Otherwise, there is nothing but the record of memory, and I know already as I wait here and watch the hooded crows that I'll remember Moscow in terms of flight. But in my notebooks I've scribbled words and impressions: food I tried for the first time (pickled garlic, caviar), the odor of spring that almost surfaced, the long line outside McDonald's. But there is nothing in those pages about wings or birds or ascent, and I will not think of such things until this trip has become a ten-year-old memory.

Irina and I have already developed two different accounts of our voyage.

"I brought you to Moscow," Irina says. "I introduced you to my friends, and you monopolized the relationships."

We came here together; Moscow was on the itinerary we both designed. I don't say that; instead, I try to explain that all I did was be myself, try to talk with people, ask them questions. But I know that every time I engaged in conversation, proffered an opinion, or responded with a less-than-ordinary, unexpected-for-an-American perspective (in other words, not mainstream media or political propaganda), Irina would give me that daggered, you're-always-on-some-other-side look, and I'd be silenced.

I look at her. *You are volatile and possessive,* I think.

The truth that I cannot point to yet, the crux of Irina's resentment, is that I am the one who grew up speaking English. Like it or not—and despite our respective abilities to navigate in Russian (Irina being the more proficient of us both, neither of us as proficient as the English-speaking Russians we meet)—it is my mother tongue, not hers, that we use here. Fluency, including my fluency in French, defines the depth of relationship with everyone we meet, and Irina has had to rely on me. She is not used to being dependent.

The ways we capture how we see Moscow are also quite different. Her photographs freeze particular moments: a cabaret singer in a white cashmere sweater and dirty white go-go boots; the empty platform at a train station. She focuses on the subject inside the frame, whereas I wander beyond the periphery of these compositions, into a short poem about the remains of worn gold letters on dishes in the restaurant where the singer performed, or a paragraph about the family huddled together under the eaves of the station saying their goodbyes before the traveler among them boards the train. These different ways of seeing the same thing define our relationship: Irina is within; I am without. I see in her a self-centeredness, a need to be in the spotlight; she perceives in me a lurk-on-the-edge quality that begs to place one toe, then the foot, finally the whole body, over the margin. In such a calculus, boundaries are transgressed. Someone will feel put out or put upon. There is no way around this.

Irina talks with Slava and Galia and her husband, Michail, all three of them Russian Jews who have welcomed us in Moscow and with whom we have spent the last four days. It is true that Irina introduced me to Galia, a woman she met in a Paris gallery and had coffee with, an encounter that ended with addresses exchanged on small pieces of paper and Galia's invitation to visit should Irina ever come to Moscow. I stand slightly apart from them, crunch a piece of dirty ice with my boot, and listen to the plans to drive to the airport. I do not participate in the confirmation of these plans because, through an unspoken agreement that has to do with Galia being Irina's "find," this last leg of the journey is Irina's responsibility. We have learned to take turns without saying "It's your turn" and to accept the decisions made by the other, even when they make us bristle, which makes me feel as though we are an unhappily married couple.

"You will take Galia's paintings out of Moscow," Michail says. His English is textbook perfect. "They are rolled up with posters of Lenin. If you should be asked questions by the border police, you will reply that Galia's paintings are merely wrappers protecting the images of Lenin."

I find this strategy clever, but recognize that I'd have a tough time explaining anything if such a conversation occurred in Russian. I want to interrupt and ask for a translation, but I know I'll forget it if I don't write it down, and how natural would that be if, once at the airport, I took out a scrap of paper with a Russian script neatly printed on it?

It's Slava who interrupts the discussion of The Plan. With his heavily accented English that has, through practice with us, improved over the last several days, he asks, "My *mufta*—how you say? . . ." He looks to Irina. *"Mufta?"*

"Embrayage," she says, looking at me.

"The car clutch?" I look at Slava. I'm taken aback that Irina knows this Russian word, and wonder if she and Slava have already struggled through the conversation we are about to have.

"My clutch . . . it is no very good, but no to worry," he says, using his hands to indicate that it's his car and he'll be driving us to the airport. His chiseled jaw seems to open and close in slow motion. Slava explains that if we leave at just the right time, he won't have to slow down or stop the vehicle because all the lights will be green, one after another. "Travel at just right speed," he adds. I picture his rusted Lada, a box with doors and wheels, the kind of car a child might draw, hurtling through the streets. But I'm unable to see myself in the backseat, nor can I imagine the laughter this ride will provoke.

As I look up at the circling crows, Galia announces that she cannot go to the airport. "I would make for you impossible to pass through the customs. I am so nervous . . . a bad actor." The other part of The Plan calls for Michail to accompany us instead, to watch as we pass through the gate, absently stroking his beard with one hand until he's certain his wife's paintings have not been confiscated. He's a tall man, and the arms of his jacket are too short, his wrists exposed.

One of Galia's watercolors is called *Preparing to Fly at Night*. With the precision of an architect, Galia has painted five rods, like those used for shower curtains. On each of these slim metallic poles hang pieces of paper—a sheet with paper airplane shapes cut out of it, another decorated with pale red crosses, several accordion-folded papers, and paper airplanes. These are not the paper airplanes of childhood, not the rapidly crimped and creased diversion that nose-dives, the kind folded and offered by adults when all the cousins under the age of six start running around the living room during the wear-and-tear hour of a family gathering. Instead, these delicate models resemble slender stingrays, attempts at flight arrested by the loops that attach them to the poles. Galia made this painting only several months before we were to take it out of Moscow to Paris, knowing, perhaps, that she would not be flying at night or at dawn or even in the afternoon. Maybe she intended this particular watercolor as a protective talisman for the rest of her work we plan to smuggle out, a postscript to all those years of painting that suggests how fragile and tenuous an idea on paper can be. Or perhaps this is Galia's way of describing all the ways she imagined leaving Moscow, all the abandoned plans for flight carefully folded into her memory. Whatever compelled Galia to paint this watercolor confirms for me the feeling I've had all along during this trip, that I'm an imposter pretending to belong to a place that was never mine.

A rim of sun breaches the horizon. I'm not sure I like having agreed to this ride in a practically clutchless vehicle. But then, what choice do I have if I am to leave Moscow as scheduled? I'd prefer to take a taxi to the airport, yet I say nothing and climb into the car. Impulse always seems to defeat reason when one attempts to leave at the time of day when edges are not distinct. Besides, these particular arrangements are Irina's to make, and she'd tell me it was rude to decline Slava's generous offer to drive us. "They can barely afford gas," she'd remind me in a tone that calls attention to my thoughtlessness. With the rolled-up paintings on my lap, I close my eyes.

Though I haven't seen or heard anything about the unraveling of the Soviet Union, a line from a Richard Wright novel keeps scratching at the back of my mind. "Most of the decisive historic events that happen in the world," he writes in *The Outsider,* "are not known until *after* they have happened." I consider these words, and how Red Square was conspicuously empty on the first of May, a national holiday in the Communist world. Everything was locked up so tight it was nearly impossible to find a place to have tea. Irina and I had wandered through the empty streets, wind riffling through the giant Soviet banners of Lenin, the sound of cloth flapping against the vacant buildings.

"There's no parade," she observed. *Rather obvious,* I thought.

"No speeches broadcast from the Kremlin," I said, considering briefly that she might think what I was saying was also quite apparent. "I feel like I'm waiting for something to happen," I said. But I left out the part about how I felt that tingling tension in the small of my back, the kind of sensation that creeps in when danger approaches from behind.

We both knew that nothing was really wrong, nor was anything really right, which described as well the state of our deteriorating friendship. And we understood the known-yet-unknown state of affairs as if we had a fused consciousness and it was this manner of understanding that had drawn Irina and me together in the first place. This merged thinking would also drive us apart, as if there weren't enough space in the same perception for both of us.

Waiting in the car for Slava and Irina and Michail, I open my eyes to the hooded crows. What are those birds looking for at this hour when the edge of a building is undefined? Anything, I guess. The unending gray feels like a shroud, which cloaks not only the mantles of the circling birds but also the pedestrian coat and cloth, grime-streaked windows, and ashen puddles.

The Italians say they invented the sun. I cannot recall where I heard that line. Why does it surface now as I prepare to leave Moscow, where I've come with a longing that has nothing to do with sunshine?

108   Kim Dana Kupperman

Under the concrete brow of the Muscovite housing projects at dawn, the daring movement of color—not the sun or its inventor—answers my question. In the grizzle of this lingering winter, I suddenly understand Chagall's lovers floating above the village, his fiddlers perched on rooftops, how he was able to join animal and human forms. And who better than Chagall, a poor Russian Jew whose father disapproved of his son's choice to make art, to declare that the color of a cloudless sky at twilight or dawn is the blue requisite for flight? And then I consider a Kandinsky painting called *Moscow 1*, how red and periwinkle and yellow fracture *and* unify that particular canvas, a picture of an exciting and turbulent city whose sky is incised with the black Vs of birds and where color itself provides light. Such vibrant tones they set down, these two painters, as if they were challenging the ambivalence of a Russia whose legacy of royalty and feudalism (and the gilded trappings) would be squeezed into the dream of class-lessness proclaimed in the Communist vision of the Soviet Union. Did they watch hooded crows circling in a muddied spring dawn and decide to fashion their own suns? "Color," Kandinsky writes, "is the power which directly influences the soul." This from a man who had abandoned a career as a successful lawyer and economist to paint.

I turn my face to the car window, where the sun is just beginning to warm the glass. Galia's paintings belong not to the Soviet state, as she had explained while rolling them up with the Lenin posters, but to a biography of color. In this narrative, she is a granddaughter who has inherited the urge to fly from Chagall, along with the certitude of Kandinsky's geometry. Yet the colors Galia uses are slate blues, olive greens, and the palest reds. Perhaps she hasn't discovered yet how to unfold the legacy of color that belongs to her. As the hooded crows circle and the sky lightens, it occurs to me that she may not be ready for such a bright and honest palette. Flight and its geometry pre-occupy Galia as much as her love of and resistance to an ambiguous homeland, a gray that she can tint, dress up in the garb of flight, but which she cannot leave.

Batman in Moscow

Six-foot dolls crowd the studio of Galia's friend Lena, who wears leather pants and tells us that her creations speak to the secret children in adults. Irina, who is here with her camera (in search of a picture she will never find), smiles and takes a photograph. As she positions her eye over the viewfinder, I wonder if she might hear the lullaby voice of Boulat Okoudjava singing a song her father played on his little tape recorder long after he had departed from Russia. "Painters," the singer implores, "dip your brushes in the tumult . . . and in the dawn."

Irina's father died many years ago and never returned to Russia once he settled in Paris. Now here is Irina, who would have been Moscow's daughter if circumstance had been altered, her feet barely touching the soil of the motherland, her finger about to release the shutter, her heart about to blink.

And here I sit, playing the American Jew who lives in Paris but who has now *come home,* though my grandparents came from what is now Ukraine. I yearn as Irina does for the sound of Russian, the throaty, rolled cadences we both heard during childhood. Filling in the blanks with English as she fills them in with French. The people we speak with nod their heads, but I know they don't understand our strange brew of vocabulary. It's as if we're held hostage by language, unable to negotiate an exchange. There's no dictionary adequate to this experience of two daughters who return to a place they've never been to and didn't come from and therefore could never have left. Yet something in both of us feels at home in this geography, longs for and somehow remembers—before we actually behold—the swirled onion domes and the buildings painted ocher, raspberry, teal . . . colors unexpected in architecture. Yet they seem perfect here, for they are the hues that saturate dreams, and they speak to me of an intense desire to overcome the long loneliness of winter.

Perhaps some form of collective memory makes us think that we should engage in return, that story we tell ourselves about going home, a story as old as storytelling itself, as ingrained as the condition of nostalgia. What price, this ticket? The fact is that I'm not home at all; I'm merely standing on ground that's been crossed in the past by strangers, some of whom were vaguely related to me. Yet during my entire stay in Moscow, the bottom of my feet tingle in a way I've never felt before, as if they were cold and hot and walking on stones that jut out of the ground. There are moments I believe that this sensation derives from transferred memory (some DNA transcription I've inherited), though at other times I imagine the streets themselves pulsing with a recall of who walked where and when. And how can language, with all its nuances and all the loss that belongs to translation, help us find what we don't know we are looking for? It's an impossible situation, I decide, to wait for some unnamed longing to be assuaged by a drench of color or the right photograph or the perfect word. The images and the language that Irina and I seek don't exist here, and, I begin to suspect, we will depart empty-handed.

Lena serves the inevitable tea from the inevitable samovar that stands on a small table in a corner of the room. Inevitable, it seems to me, because of the real or imagined samovars in every Chekhov play I've ever seen or read, as if the afternoon tea service that endured even as Lenin came to power had an inherent right to be preserved across time and shifting political regimes and borders. With the cups, Lena brings a lemon, a knife, and a chipped, rose-patterned dish piled with sugared cranberries.

The dolls surround us, all with red mouths stretched into permanent smiles, corn yellow shoulder-length hair, and pale skin daubed pink on the cheeks. These are not colors inherited from painters like Chagall or Kandinsky. Rather, the dolls remind me of some Aryan reverie gone awry, a small army of blondes at the ready, but for what I have no idea. Looking at them for too long raises the hair on the back of my neck. I'm impatient to leave Lena's studio, but it wouldn't be polite, and besides, Irina and I are bound by our foreignness and prior agreement to circulate together. I sip my tea quietly, wondering what secret child would be attracted to such grotesque mannequins. I want to tell Lena that those who feel lost as children—and by this I mean severed from place, or understanding at an early age that home is a false conceit and always temporary—might not harbor a secret child. Irina sets down the camera and stirs her tea. I eat a sugared cranberry, the confection smooth and sweet and powdery on the outside, tart and surprising in its liquidity inside. The tea, the candy, and the samovar belong here, in my sepia-toned inner picture of Russia, but the dolls seem out of place, as if child's play—secret or otherwise—is impossible to locate in this Soviet world.

And so how should I think of the thing I had seen that morning through the hotel window, painted in white on the roof of the building below? A Batman insignia, an icon of my own after-school childhood, not big or flashy like the one Commissioner Gordon used to alert the superhero, projecting the image into the low clouds of Gotham City, but outlined on a rooftop like a call for help. Who was calling for Batman in Moscow? And why? It couldn't have been children who made that image, more likely that young adults, enamored of all things Western, painted it. I look around at the life-size dolls mounted on the walls, propped up against the windows, seated in chairs. When Irina came to the window to see the outline of bat wings, she remarked that American culture has no sense of boundary. "It spreads everywhere, like a cancer," she said. I agreed with her, mostly to diffuse the growing tension between us, to quell my gut reaction that her comment was really directed at me. But also because I really agreed.

Now, sitting in Lena's studio, I realize how much I'd like to signal Batman, watch him crash through the window and destroy these dolls, rescue me from the clutches of bad art and spoiled friendship. ("Holy mannequins, Batman," I hear Robin say as superhero and protégé stand on the broken glass, their capes settling with a crinkle.) What a waste of time that would be. Lena would just make more six-foot creatures, and in less than a year her studio would be filled with them again. But I imagine the scene anyway, Batman with a red cape and speaking Russian, arriving in the nick of time.

"Comrades . . . ," he says. Just the thought of that word coming from his mouth makes the fantasy vanish. Feeling like I might laugh, I pretend to hide a burp with the back of my hand.

Irina looks at me and for a moment I see—in the way her mouth is set in a stony and ancient perpetuity, how her gaze settles on some point behind my head—that she has considered the many uses, including harm to me, of the pearl-handled knife balanced on the edge of the plate with the lemon.

"Would you like some vodka?" Lena asks.

I decline. There are no bat-eared masked men around, only six-foot dolls, a tall woman with big hands and leather pants, and Irina hiding behind her Leica.

And I am very far away from home, no more returned than when I first landed in Moscow.

Aborted Flight

The attraction between Slava and Irina manifests when we arrive in Moscow, first as a flashing back and forth of the eyes, then as a practically tangible heat produced as they stand next to each other. I know that the ensuing flirtation means I will barely be able to talk with Slava, and so I try to blend into the background.

He takes Irina and me to a Goya exhibit and I feel like the little sister tagging along on a date, instructed beforehand to be quiet and nonpresent. The small museum is almost empty, allowing us to stand so close to the etchings that we might smell the paper if glass didn't protect them. Goya had already lost his hearing when he completed this series, *Los Desastres de la Guerra,* which would not be printed until after he died. My great-grandmother, who was deaf, always said she'd rather have been blind, that the silence she inhabited was desolate, and she longed to hear the music she danced to, music whose vibrations she sensed in her feet. In front of these etchings by Goya, I wonder if deafness sharpened his eye, or if it moved him to feel and depict a more profound loneliness. Or if it did both.

We face an image that depicts three figures—a soldier initiating the rape of a young woman, who digs her fingers into his face while burying her head in his opposite shoulder, and an old woman raising a dagger behind the man's back. Because of the tall furlike hat he wears, the soldier resembles a Cossack, though *Los Desastres de la Guerra* documented Napoleon's invasion of Portugal and Spain during the Peninsular War of 1808–1814. In spite of the mismatched geography and time, the likeness between the French soldier and a Cossack, along with the subject matter, situates this particular picture for me in the czarist Russia of my grandparents, who lived at the time of the pogroms, when the rape of women by soldiers occurred so frequently that Jewish families hid their daughters in pickle barrels.

The title of this particular etching, *No quieren* (They Do Not Want To), seems odd in its use of the third person plural. Though the action is suspended and the characters have not opened their mouths to demand or protest, there is something very auditory in this etching, something vernacular in the expression *They do not want to,* something fill-in-the-blank about it. I can almost hear the crumple of the young woman's billowy dress against the soldier's coarse uniform, can almost hear the light step taken by the old woman before she moves forward with the raised knife.

As I puzzle out what Goya might have meant by the title, I overhear Slava asking Irina, "Maybe you consider marriage me . . . so I can leave this place?"

She does not answer. I wonder if Slava thinks she is feigning deafness. The creases in the corners of his eyes wet up, and I imagine him moved to tears by the strength and insistence of Irina's profile. I know better: for Slava the Russian Jew, there are only two choices where flight is concerned—immigrate to Israel or marry a foreign-born Jew.

Perhaps, though, he thinks Irina hasn't fully understood his question, which he has asked in his imperfect English. Maybe he feels as if he's used the wrong part of speech or an incorrect verb. Here at the museum, Irina and I have abandoned our dictionary and wander instead through the language with spontaneity and gesture, looking at the ceiling when we cannot remember a word. It's not that Irina wouldn't accommodate Slava's departure, but that she cannot visualize his arrival in her world. She is a private woman who lives with a dog named Pushkin. Her bathroom serves as a darkroom more often than not, and there is no space on her shelves for the books or belongings of another. Even her friends do not just drop in; she expects them to call at least a week ahead and make a date.

Is that what Goya was after with this etching—making us feel not only complicit, as witnesses who do not intervene are, but also as if we are intruders? The empty space between Slava's question and Irina's silence lingers and expands, and I cannot dissolve it even when I exhale loud enough for them to hear.

Galia invites us to her place to celebrate our last night in Moscow. Two of her neighbors, a young man and a young woman, join us and bring a guitar. We sit around the kitchen table, Lena at one corner with a tumbler of vodka in her large hand, Slava at another corner staring out the window. Michail washes glasses, holding each one up to the light for inspection. Galia passes out dishes and little forks. Irina fiddles with her camera.

The tension between Irina and me erupted this morning in our hotel room. I was glad for the relief that is felt when things come to a head and you think the air will clear afterward.

"You intrude on my friendships," she said.

"What do you mean?" I asked.

"You know exactly what I mean. First, Galia. All your questions about art. Then Slava. I see how you look at him."

"Irina, I honestly don't . . ."

I was looking out the window as I said this, at the Batman insignia sketched on the tar-papered roof.

"You are lying. You know exactly what I'm talking about. Ever since we got here, you've tried to be close to Galia, offering to make a connection for her in New York, or to translate a catalog. Ever since we came to the Soviet Union, in fact, you've always tried to talk to people I was interested in."

"Irina, I'm the one whose language is used here. I was merely acting as an interpreter for both of us. And I thought if I talked to Galia, it'd give you some time alone with Slava."

"I don't need you to organize my relationships," Irina said.

Two people carrying buckets and mops appeared on the rooftop. I wanted to bang on the window, smash the glass really, and yell, "Stop!" Though it was ridiculous, I wanted that Batman signal to stay right where it was, a perennial call for help.

"I wasn't organizing anything. I was only trying . . ."

"You think because you're Jewish, like me or like Galia or Slava, that we're supposed to automatically like and protect one another. Let me tell you something—you're an American Jew, which gives you a different attitude, a different way of walking through the world. For us Europeans, it's quite different, and not something you'll ever understand, no matter how many questions you ask."

Sitting in Galia's kitchen, I am barely able to look at Irina without clenching my jaw.

"You know Vladimir Vysotsky?" the young man asks in English. "He is dead but I play for you his songs. He is like a hero." He tunes his guitar, plucks a rapid, folksy melody, and then stops to eat a pickled tomato.

Slava raises his head. "Vysotsky was . . . how you say? *Bard,* like Okoudjava. He played Hamlet."

The bard who played the prince of Denmark? I usually resist such lofty metaphors, suspicious of how they reside in a collective memory nostalgic for a time or movement that might not have existed. Maybe it's the vodka, cool on my throat and warm in my chest, which allows me to believe what's being said about this dead poet who resisted authority.

"Brezhnev once remarked that the air in Moscow would be more breathable if both Okoudjava and Vysotsky stopped breathing," Galia says.

Irina smiles. Slava looks at her. I try to be as inconspicuous as possible. My teeth hurt. Since words have failed me up to this point, I do not say anything. But I wonder what it feels like for Irina, who is usually the beholder, the one whose eye takes things in and freezes them, to be, as she is for Slava, the beheld.

The young man begins to sing as though he were Vysotsky, his voice rough with cigarette smoke and a life lived mostly on the cold streets, an existence warmed with too much alcohol and made thin by too little to eat. I'll learn later that evening how much he sounds like Vysotsky when Galia plays an old LP on an even older record player, the kind I had as a child. And before I see the hooded crows or the dawn, I'll realize that this entire adventure in Moscow is nothing but an excursion into other people's attempts at departure.

The young man plays a riff between verses.

"This song is called 'Aborted Flight,'" his companion says. She leans over to tell me this, and she's so close that I smell a salt dampness in her hair, as though she might have cried before coming here tonight.

In Galia's kitchen, Slava and Michail pour vodka from bottles with no labels. Lena passes the jars of pickled garlic and tomatoes, as if dishing out the bounty of last summer's garden. There's practically no soil or greenery in these concrete suburbs of Moscow, but a century ago, vegetables probably grew here. I close my eyes, and for an instant, I'm in a kitchen warm with bodies and scented with sweat and vinegar, in a house that stood here one hundred summers past.

And the music of a dead poet—"like a Russian Bob Dylan," the young man exclaims—takes wing above the wooden roof of this imagined house and the abundance of the garden. In spite of the concrete that has replaced it.

Preparing to Fly at Dawn

The hooded crows perch and caw like sentinels. I think of Poe's raven as illogical here. Or is it? I feel oddly comforted by the word *nevermore,* reminded that the business of returning to a place that doesn't belong to me is impossible.

I want to ask Irina if she believes she'll see Galia again, if she thinks she and Slava might marry, if there's any chance we'll recapture the excitement we had when we first made these plans to travel together to Russia. I know, however, that Irina and I will arrive in Paris and go our separate ways, that this trip to Moscow has dissolved whatever friendship we pretended, that we are pretending even now to not have failed.

What I don't know is that once I'm home in my small apartment in Paris, in three months I'll be listening to news on the radio about the August 19 coup, which leads to the collapse of the Soviet Union by the end of that year. By September, after Gorbachev is placed under house arrest and then released, I'll write to a friend and quote Richard Wright. "I stood on the edge of History," I'll tell anyone who'll listen, though I won't be sure of what that means exactly. For weeks after I leave Moscow, I'll dream of Russia. Not this Russia that I'm leaving at dawn, but a place pieced together from swatches of Chagall's blue, inevitable samovars, and the amber tones of etchings that transgress temporal and physical borders. I'll scribble small notes to myself, to remember, for example, the pigeons at the monastery at Zagorsk, and the old, bent woman in black who fed them.

The sun bleeds into my eyes as I watch Galia wave good-bye.

Galia of the walnut hair cut at a slant just above her jaw. Galia wearing a plum sweater over a chartreuse turtleneck and a cobalt skirt that falls to her ankles. Galia dressed in the speaking tongues of watercolors she has yet to paint. As the car pulls away, I wave back. Galia's hand recedes, then fades.

Slava drives, sailing through every intersection, all the lights green as he had predicted. Irina rides shotgun, and I see a lightness, a buoyancy, in the back of her head that I don't expect, but which allows me to relax my jaw, and gives me a vague hope that we might repair what is broken between us, if not now, perhaps in years to come.

The streets of Moscow are empty at dawn, and we laugh all the way to the airport.

return to sender

four points

I learned that there is a poetry in distances, that yearning could be
a higher plane, lightly stimulated by painful borders.
David Lazar, *The Body of Brooklyn*

Departure

At 1:30 AM on April 9, 1986, the year that Halley's Comet was last visible from Earth, the planes rested in shadow outside Paris's Orly Airport. None departed, none arrived. The moon, still new, could not be seen, so it was by the glow of off-hours lights inside the terminus that the noses and wings of the airplanes outside were vaguely outlined. Inside, the fluorescence from blue and yellow signs bounced off the polished floors and stuck to the window. Like the white of an egg, the airport interior was viscous. It contained departure, waiting, arrival.

Philippe and I had arrived at Orly with the intention of leaving France.

Earlier that evening, we had dined at his aunt's boyfriend's apartment, where Philippe was staying for several days. The boyfriend, Léon Charles, was out of town. The aunt, Marie-Christine, lived in another part of the city. I was never clear on why Philippe was in Paris. Probably he was on break from the university where he was a student in Montpellier. He came from the eastern part of France, the Franche-Comté, where I had first met him, and where I had been a student and where I still maintained an apartment and a relationship, both of which were deteriorating in different ways. The flat had a leaky roof, cracked windows, and insufficient heat. My boyfriend had no such flaws—he was smart, funny, and handsome, but he was young and unready to commit. Philippe was almost done with being nineteen, and I, at twenty-six (going on what I thought was thirty-six), played the Older Woman to his barely twentyness. All we really knew about each other was that he was a biology student, and I taught English and wrote poetry.

In the apartment of the absent Léon Charles, we made a feast of cucumber salad, hard Comté cheese, a baguette, and a bottle of white from the Arbois. As the night edged into late, we talked about leaving France.

"No more exams—sounds good to me," he said. "I'm ready."

"No more teaching French businessmen the finer points of the English verb," I answered. I pictured my clients, looking at their watches, wondering where I was, not daring to imagine such recklessness on my part.

We can look back on this night when we are older, I thought, knowing that regardless of the rash departure we were planning, I was headed straight for an adulthood defined by routine.

Ten minutes later, we were out the door.

I carried a black leather satchel. Inside the zippered front pocket, I kept a date book with a cartoonish picture of Halley's Comet on the cover and pages that documented where I had been and how I had arrived there. That year of the comet, my compulsion with details had reached its own cosmological height. I admit now that there's something to be said for having recorded so much information, to know, for example, that on March 3, 1986, I walked to the Eiffel Tower with a friend, watched the lights illuminate it at nightfall, and had a quick drink at a Viennese café; afterward I met my roommate for dinner. My shoulder was stiff, the weather was cold, and my English classes lasted three hours that day. I packed my bag for a trip home to Besançon. Other entries reveal whom I had seen or talked with, letters I had written, and correspondences received. If I went to the cinema or watched a film on television, if I read a book or an article, I wrote it down. Perhaps because the heavens were so busy that year (with the comet and two eclipses), I also noted the astrological house I entered each month.

In the larger pocket of my bag lodged the other ephemera that clung to me then: a second notebook with descriptions of dreams, notes, and bad poetry neatly inked onto its pages; an *International Herald Tribune* folded to the crossword puzzle; a pack of cigarettes, a lighter, and a box of matches; a bottle of aspirin; a wallet organizing my identification papers and meager funds; a hairbrush; a pair of clean underwear; and a soft pouch containing a bottle of Wite-Out, highlighters, a Waterman pen, and a red and white Altoids peppermint tin filled with blue-black ink cartridges.

I wore black velvet and a sapphire blue scarf.

Philippe was more practical at traveling lightly. He tucked a slim wallet into the back pocket of his jeans and carried a bottle of Armagnac, which bulged in the deep recesses of a long black coat. He reminded me of a drifter in a black-and-white Western. He seemed transported through time—he should have been, I thought, a contemporary of Mozart's—and this enchanted me. I believed then that I had been dropped into the world several hundred years too late.

In the taxi to Orly, I dipped my fingers underneath the fold of his pocket. I sat so close to Philippe that I smelled the cucumbers and crisp Arbois—*summer,* I thought—on his breath. The feel of the bottle inside his coat raised memories of childhood beaches and the surprises that lay upon the sand: sea- and sand-worn glass, sunrise shells, the abandoned shelters of horseshoe crabs. *We are doing this,* I told myself, though I didn't want to fully believe it, *leaving the city, leaving the treachery of quotidian habit. We will be breathing different air tomorrow. Together.*

We entered the airport determined to fly anywhere in the just-new morning, a leather satchel and a bottle of Armagnac as our sole luggage, complicit in our abandon.

"We'll have a new life," Philippe said. "In Africa or Sweden."

"Whichever flight comes first," I promised.

We waited for the ticket counters to open; we waited for the sun to rise. We didn't really have a plan, just an idea about departure. We waited for the partial eclipse of the sun, scheduled to occur around four that morning. We waited to be airborne as the sun passed through shadow. Whatever came first. We hardly knew each other but it didn't matter because we both wanted to leave Paris, if only for a night, though we said words like *forever* and *at least a year*. We indulged what we considered our last chance to break free—from the path of our fathers and mothers and aunts and uncles and distant cousins, all of whom seemed to work for this company or that school or any number of organizations, from nonprofits to governmental agencies—and be insubordinate to rules, to act as impetuously and foolishly as we dared, to admit that we did not really care about whom or what we left behind. To play as children trapped in adult bodies.

We chatted with airport janitors taking a coffee break. These men from Cameroon spoke to us in the formal French learned in classrooms, only their accents rose and fell like the lilt and song of tropical mountains. *A place of wild parrots*, I thought, *a place I might like*. The men stood in a circle, shifting their weight from foot to foot, as if they were involuntarily dancing, or as if their feet were remembering a dance no longer performed. Their skin was rendered chartreuse in the glare of signs directing travelers—who would materialize once the morning began in earnest—in, out, and to planes.

"Where are you going?" one of them asked.

"Anywhere," Philippe said.

"As far away as we can go on the first flight out," I added.

"Maybe you should go to where we come from," one of the men said, and I wondered if we might just do that.

He threw his head back and laughed. Because I believed that anything was possible in a year when you could see Halley's Comet, especially on a day when an eclipse was going to occur, I half expected orchids to bloom from his open, upturned mouth. I was that hopeful back then, or perhaps I was desperate for a bit of sorcery in a world that looked increasingly less magical.

When the men dispersed, we walked away and found a place to sit and wait. Philippe set the bottle of Armagnac on the table. He fixed his eyes on my face.

An asymmetric geometry arched Philippe's left brow. The color of his eyes reminded me of how swallows cut the dusk—and its notion of wild irises—into shreds. "His mouth," I would write later in my notebook, "must have been fashioned by an alchemist of mouths. In the creases of his lips, I detect the dormant shadows of other centuries. His hair: an adagio of brown curls."

"What are you looking for?" I asked.

"You," Philippe replied. This was exactly the sort of answer I wanted.

He stood, extended his hand. We took off our shoes and danced in socks and silence, gliding under the blue and yellow lights on the polished floor of an empty airport. The building seemed to glow on the outside as it did inside, eclipsing its own shadow.

"If music *were* to play," he said, "it would be Mozart." *Naturellement.* And of course I heard it then—strains of "A Little Night Music," a melody I would later hum under my breath while waiting tables during the lunch rush in a rotisserie in Midtown Manhattan that catered to businessmen. I'd teach English to the men in suits on one side of the Atlantic, feed them French food on the other.

I traced the V-shaped scar on Philippe's cheek. His fingers spread long and cool on my waist. We danced like that until he said he was thirsty, and then we returned to the table and each took a swig from the bottle.

We roamed the airport, looked through the windows of the closed shops, walked outside to gaze at the stars, then came inside, sat in the terminal's blue plastic chairs, and waited. I realized then that we would not be traveling anywhere, at least not by airplane. But it didn't matter; the *attempt* to leave, to escape futures we didn't want, was what mattered. I know now that I was helping Philippe rehearse for his final, dramatic exit, but as we sat in the chairs at Orly, when he laid his head in my lap, I had secured the departure I had wanted when we hatched our plan to leave Paris. The airport lights blinked on like a giant eye.

Arrival

The fluorescent sunrise inside the airport reminded me that arrival requires departure. At 4:09 AM on April 9, the partial eclipse of the sun began, and it was at this exact moment (not only did I look at the terminal clock, I recorded the time in my Halley's Comet date book) that I bent my head, closed my eyes, and kissed Philippe. He tasted like a long summer day where one hour becomes the next and exasperated parents call you out of the water—*Your lips are turning blue*—and the beach is infinite and full of surprises. He smelled like copper and butter, and as soon as my mouth met his, I knew I had arrived and departed at the same time, and that I would return over and over to the metal and cream of this memory. It wasn't the chemical attraction that I recall now, but the sheer luck and excitement of touching a visitor from another dimension. That's what Philippe seemed to me, a man-boy cobbled together from Hollywood Westerns and distant centuries, with dusk for eyes and music for hair.

I expected to recall each piece of that morning, as if our failed attempt at flight had been transformed into something else, childhood's end, perhaps, or a boundary of age that we stepped over with deliberate insolence. Instead, my memories are much more concrete: we left the airport on a bus, Philippe's head on my shoulder, my hand in his pocket, his eyes closed, mine on the sky, which did not darken since this eclipse was not visible in Paris. But I perceived a kind of moving shadow in the air, and I would recognize its effects later, looking at a photograph of Philippe, a picture I took before he died.

We watched people come and go, strangers who bustled on the streets toward invisible destinations. Where they were headed didn't matter; their presence—something about the anonymity of each human being in a waking world—confirmed we were living a moment that would dangle unhinged, like any secret that detaches from memory.

I followed Philippe as he climbed the flight of shining wooden stairs to Léon Charles's fifth-floor apartment.

The sun stormed through the bedroom window, an amber violence that streaked Philippe's bare flesh with bands of honeyed light. I knew I had to let him touch my wrist like he was taking my pulse, that I had to visit, if only once, this place he had opened. I felt weightless, as if I were shadow.

"*Vous êtes experte, Madame,*" Philippe said hours later, once gravity had been restored.

Was that really what he told me? I did not record it in my notebook.

When I left later that morning, Philippe was sleeping, half covered by the twisted sheets, the breeze billowing a chintz curtain. Clouds had obscured the sun and a light rain started to fall. I returned in the afternoon and we listened to records (Mozart), danced, ate cheese, and talked. The next night, his aunt invited us to dinner at her apartment. Marie-Christine was ten years older than I was then and ten years younger than I am now. She was intrigued by her nephew, happy to see him bring a woman to dinner. We all went out for drinks. It rained. Philippe stood up suddenly and left the bar. His absence was so complete that he might as well have left the solar system. Marie-Christine shook her head.

"He does that sometimes," she told me. "Stomps off like a hurt little boy." But none of us knew, or would ever know, what had been said to offend him.

I tried the next night to see Philippe, but he had left Paris. Though it required great concentration, I resumed teaching English during the week and returning to my apartment and boyfriend on the weekends, leaving this routine whenever I was able.

Return

A month after our night at Orly, I visited Philippe in Montpellier, where he attended university. We played tag on the beach. He picked me up and threw me into the sea. My great-grandmother's watch, clasped on my left wrist, stopped when I hit the water. I chased and caught Philippe and carried him into the shallow waves. He felt unbearably light and I wondered how it had come to be that I was living that moment in exactly that way. Until I took that watch to be repaired, it read 4:09, a strange reminder of our attempted flight. Every time I looked at its face, I saw myself drenched and laughing, arrested in that moment, as if it were the point of departure from which I would always be willing to leave everything behind for an adventure that never happened, only to return to its memory.

We sat on the sand, towels draped over our wet heads. Philippe talked about the promise of hot chocolate in a nearby café, but all I thought about was staring into the dusk of his eyes. Instead, I took his photograph.

The last time I saw Philippe, he came to visit me in New York City a year after he had thrown me into the water and stopped time. Ambling with him in the autumn evening, I felt my pulse quicken. I'd been surprised when he called from a pay phone and asked if I would meet him at the corner.

"If you don't," he said, "I'll go to Coney Island instead."

"I'll be right down," I said.

Before I hung up the telephone, I calculated the distance between us—four floors and half a city block. Under the streetlights of the city where I was once a child, he stared into my eyes, his face so close I smelled the summer on his breath.

"I don't think you're real," I told him.

He took my hand, turned it palm up. Over my life line he placed a paper clip and then he folded my fingers closed around it.

"I'm as light as paper," he whispered.

We walked down Columbus Avenue. I chattered—about how I had missed him, and how we should visit the Museum of Natural History—and he was mostly silent. I wanted to hold him, to kiss him again, to suggest we revisit our effort at leaving the life I was starting to make in New York, a life of waiting tables and sleeping late and writing poems I cannot bear to look at now, a life that would mutate into a series of different jobs, lovers, deaths of close relations, moves between France and America, an epistolary life that I would describe to friends and family in missives sent from home and abroad. He walked me to the door of my building. When we said good-bye, his fingers spread long and cool on the nape of my neck and when he kissed me, I tasted his smell of copper and butter and felt time stopping at 4:09 in the morning in a distant airport and at 4:09 in the afternoon on a faraway beach.

Vanishing Point

I was in Paris three years later when a friend told me that Philippe had killed himself. For his suicide he returned home to the eastern mountains of France and on Mother's Day rode a bicycle off a waterfall. He left no messages. His room was tidy—the bed made, books stacked on his desk. The bicycle was never recovered.

There are times when I am not convinced that our adventure at the Orly Airport really occurred, as if my memory has obscured the facts. These collected and re-collected moments with Philippe—the attempted departure to distant lands, the arrival in the lean country of his flesh, the drenched shoreline of stopped watches, the walk on a street in the city I was born in and returned to—are all I have. I would write about that eclipse over and over again so that what I knew of Philippe (the viscous light of the airport, the indelible dusk in his eyes) would not disappear after I forgot such details as the color of my apartment walls, or a home telephone number or street address.

I wonder now if I sensed that Philippe felt, as they say in French, "bad" in his skin, though I was more inclined to believe that he was not of this world. Even his hair was ethereal. I was afraid to say he might have been an apparition (spirit . . . angel . . . ghost . . . messenger), but I always smiled when I thought of the possibility.

After my friend told me the news and I had returned home, I dug out the picture of Philippe, made the day he tossed me in the water. The photo is underexposed, as if a shadow had eclipsed the lens when the shutter closed. But I could still discern those eyes and that mouth underneath the fuzzy haze.

I even sensed myself on the other side of that picture, yearning for a point of departure. The slight weight of a paper clip still in my pocket.

the perfect meal

Scientists found that food tastes better when you're hungry.
   Harper's, "Findings," May 2004

Quentin and I wait for our cheeseburgers in the fancy hotel restaurant. We're both a little shaky from that blood-sugar edge that comes when you're hungry and you've spent the last three hours kissing someone you've wanted to kiss for three months but couldn't because you live too far away from each other and are both married.

"Do you know," he asks me, "that of the sixty-five people executed in 2003, ten ate cheeseburgers as their last meal?"

It's the odd piece of information he'd know, and I feel a mix of delight and melancholy over Quentin's ability to recite the last meals of death-row inmates.

Maybe it's silly to be moved by someone's command of bizarre trivia, but my eyes are beginning to moisten, and the last thing I want to do is cry into a beige napkin in a hotel dining room. The melodrama of tears in public annoys me and I don't want to blow my strong-and-capable-woman cover in front of Quentin. Besides, I know there'll be plenty of crying when we say good-bye to each other three days from now. I blink back the tears.

"How many ate seafood?" I ask. I'd request Oysters Rockefeller or mussels steamed in white wine, the kinds of things I would never cook at home because they're too complicated and messy, and all those shells in the trash mean raccoons pillaging after midnight in my rural Maine backyard.

"Eleven. Seven had fried fish. Only one guy ordered linguini with white clam sauce. Another asked for shrimp, but the prison kitchen didn't have any so he ate snacks from the vending machine."

When he smiles, fine lines fan from the corners of Quentin's eyes, beyond the rim of his glasses. From conversations we've had over the last three months about all the ways we've been cheated by the world—from insurance company scams to having invented something that someone else gets the credit for—I know what he's thinking, and I'm thinking the same thing, that requesting a final meal that can't be prepared or delivered is exactly what would happen to both of us.

In the basement of a community college, Quentin runs a small press and makes hand-bound books.

"I'd spend all my time underground if I didn't have to support my family. Feed myself out of the vending machines," he once told me. He moonlights as a clown on the birthday-party circuit, and works a day job at Barnes & Noble.

Such a bookstore is the most unlikely place for two people who construct handmade books to meet. I hate franchises of any sort, especially those that sell books on paper that doesn't last. And so does Quentin, but he needs the money.

I was visiting my friend Dorrie last summer.

"There's a reading at Barnes & Noble," she said. "Supposed to be a pretty good writer." She knows how much I despise megabookstore chains, and I probably rolled my eyes when she suggested we go, but we went anyway. When it was time for the novelist to read, a total of nine people had gathered. Quentin, the assistant manager, was one of them. He stood next to me.

"I always feel sorry for these guys," he said. "They travel far, read to a dozen people more or less. Then we remainder their books in a couple of months."

"And the cruelest part," I said, "is that their books will disintegrate in twenty years."

"Too much acid in the paper," we said at the same time. Both of us speaking under our breath, a habit I have when I don't want to appear as if I know too much, something Quentin does because he's shy and knows a lot. That's all it took for me to look at Quentin a little more closely, the odd coincidence of two strangers realizing at the same moment that they already know something about one another.

After the reading, the novelist invited everyone for a round of drinks. I didn't really want to go, but Dorrie had her eyes on that writer, and when Quentin said his shift was about to end and asked if I'd be joining them, the idea suddenly seemed appealing.

"I like your hair," he said.

I felt myself blush.

"I was thinking of cutting it. It's kind of a pain, and with my large head and all this hair, it's hard to find a hat that fits," I said.

God, Kim, you are a moron. Clearly, I had forgotten how to flirt, and wasn't that what I was supposed to be doing as I sipped my drink and talked to an assistant manager at Barnes & Noble who had just told me he liked my hair?

"Don't," he said. He leaned toward me and our arms touched.

Three months later and we're attending a book arts workshop on traditional bindings, in a city neither of us has ever been to, which seems fitting since neither of us has ever done what we're doing now—talking about the final meals of dead men in a fancy hotel restaurant far away from our homes and spouses. Over cheeseburgers.

There are many ways to bind a book, but the codex—with its hard covers, hand-sewn signatures, and endpapers—is the most familiar binding. Because the codex is one of the hardest bindings to master, it's the one that most satisfies me. Patience and exactitude are the hallmarks of the well-constructed codex. You must measure twice and cut once. Stand perfectly still while pulling the blade through the paper lest the movement of the body disturb the hand. The paste has to dry overnight. All the parts need to line up exactly. If there's the tiniest spot of glue on a finger, a cover may be ruined. You learn to hold your breath, to see in increments of sixteenths and thirty-seconds of inches, to wait.

For me, making a book is the only way to be still. When I write, I leave my desk every fifteen minutes (and before sitting down to write, I clean the house and wash the dishes); when I talk on the phone, I pace; when I cook, I talk on the phone. When I love someone, I want everything to happen All At Once. Quentin is the opposite—for him, time is an opportunity to unfold himself slowly.

"I'm pushing fifty," Quentin says. I already know he's forty-seven, though he'd look late thirties if his hair were more pepper than salt.

Pushing, I think, trying to dismiss the image that the tall man sitting with me is playing the role of Sisyphus toiling behind a rock, that he's dressed in a toga and sandals. What does it mean to push an age? Are we pushing it away from us, pushing toward it, pushing beyond its range or the expectations attached to it? Wearing a leather flight jacket that he bought at a flea market for five dollars, Quentin looks like the kind of man who wouldn't have to push anything to get what he wants. He's lean and muscular, has the long fingers of a pianist, and it took all of thirty seconds for him to pull me close to him, take my hair in his hand, and lean down to kiss me.

Still visible on his jacket are the previous owner's initials, *KFC*.

Quentin loves the novelty of someone having the same initials as Kentucky Fried Chicken, but as his eyes narrow, I see he's also troubled.

"What do you think his name was, Kevin Franklin Connor? Keith Frederick Churchill? Who gives children the kinds of initials they'll get teased about? Who does that to their kids?" Quentin asks me.

"I don't have children," I remind him.

It would have been something to have made and named a baby with Quentin, I think, realizing that what's happening to me here is much more than extramarital kissing. I close that thought as if it were a curtain I'd rather not look behind, and imagine instead watching Quentin play basketball with his daughter, or the look on his face as he points to a painting his son just completed. I respect this man's devotion to his children, how his voice softens and his shoulders drop when he talks about them. And it saddens me too that I'll never know Quentin's kids more than the stories he tells about them, or the pictures he digs out of his wallet to show me.

Quentin's wedding band is simple compared to his complicated watch, which has all kinds of buttons and lights, a timepiece he never removes because if he did, he might forget to put it on again. He's not the kind of man you'd picture eating a twelve-dollar cheeseburger and drinking a seven-dollar beer at three thirty in the afternoon, sitting with a woman who is not his wife. Then again, what kind of man would you picture? Would he be an investment banker in a three-piece suit with a fourteen-karat Rolex? Order sherry or cognac instead of beer? A used-car salesman trying to hide a bald spot with a comb-over, a DJ who sports a ponytail? A guy who covers up a paunch with a fashionable blazer, or announces his virility with an open shirt that reveals a gold chain nestled in his chest hair? A high roller who pays for your meal with a wad of cash instead of asking the waiter for separate checks?

"I don't want to be," Quentin says, "the cliché of a married man who sits at the bar and says his wife doesn't understand him."

Quentin is no cliché. What bartender would expect a clown who binds and sells books to confess to a marriage that's lost its humor, its binding, its story? Look at me. Almost forty-five and I refuse to believe that I'm playing a pre-scripted role: the middle-aged (but young-looking) married woman whose sexual self is awakened after a decade of dormancy, who's willing to challenge her own notions of what's right to feel alive. I've just spent the afternoon fulfilling a desire that's been forged over the course of lengthy phone calls and in elaborate letters precisely printed on handmade paper. Do I seem like *that* kind of woman—hair in slight disarray, lips a little swollen, one earring missing? Or do I have an air of seriousness that says *Look, don't touch,* the tough demeanor of a film noir heroine—Simone Signoret or Marlene Dietrich—whose coiffure never strays and who can walk down cobbled streets in stilettos without spraining her ankle? A woman who'd tell a married man, in a voice that sounds like smoke and honey, "Call me when you figure out what you really want."

No cheeseburger has ever tasted this good. Broiled—his medium, mine medium rare—with evenly melted cheddar, the soft buns toasted just enough. The plates are garnished with lettuce, tomato, onion, and sour pickles. The meat is succulent, the patties not too thick or thin. Quentin eats the onion, which I'll smell on his breath later when we walk around and find a fountain. There he'll put on his red clown nose and take two pennies from his pocket.

"Make a wish," he'll say.

I'll laugh, the wind will pick up, and spray from the fountain will dampen my face and hair. I won't mind the odor of onion that lingers when I kiss Quentin into the early hours of the morning because my wish, of course, was to do just that, kiss him again.

The cheeseburger tastes earthy and smoky, more like something mined from the earth than cut from an animal that walked aboveground and ate grass and oats. Or maybe it's that I feel like I'm biting into a memory I need to preserve in order to feel more human, a memory packed in salt, as Yeats said, something whose taste I know will never be the same without Quentin there to share it with me.

I'm not sure I seem like the kind of woman who eats cheeseburgers, though it's hard to say what cheeseburger-eating women look like. Are they long-haired and narrow around the waist as I am? Do they look, as someone once told me, like they've been eating apples (not beef) all their lives? Are they sorry about the closing of the gap between their front teeth? Did they inherit high cheekbones from their mothers? The stereotypical cheeseburger-eating women are most likely over-weight, dressed in polyester, with bleached-blonde hair and exposed roots, more likely to be sighted in a McDonald's with their children in tow. Do you think you'd see one in Burger King with a man she'd been kissing—not her husband—for three hours?

My friends understand that I'm particular about food, where it comes from, how it's prepared and served. At home I buy organic, free-range meat. I purchase my staples from a co-op, try to grow and preserve as many of my own vegetables as possible. I write educa-tional materials for farmers in my community; the only activism I'm involved in these days has to do with food. I've waited on tables and worked in kitchens off and on for half my adult life, and have stan-dards about what I eat. I never consume fast or processed foods. If my friends could see me now, they might be disappointed that I'd be unable to pinpoint the origin of my cheeseburger.

"When I used to wait on tables," I say, "I hated doing the ketchup."

"What do you mean?"

I'm not sure why I'm telling this story, except that I'm holding a bottle of Heinz and it's filled to the top and very clean. Maybe I'd like Quentin to know that I once dirtied my bookmaking hands with food, the same hands I keep clean to handle paper, the ones I've spent three months moisturizing so they'd be soft when I touched him. Per-haps it's just the act of coaxing ketchup onto my cheeseburger that's connected me to a job from the past. Or the easy intimacy of linking the Now of Quentin with the Then of my unmarried, you-wouldn't-catch-me-with-a-married-man, less complicated self.

"At the end of a shift, we'd fill the ketchup bottles by turning them upside down on top of each other. Then we'd wipe the bottle necks and inside the caps," I explain. "It was messy."

He takes a bite of his cheeseburger. I take a bite of mine.

"I'd drive you crazy. I make messes when I cook," Quentin says. "Take whatever's in the fridge and put it all together, hope for a beautiful accident."

I'm startled by this. Quentin doesn't like surprises. He drives a standard to have greater control. He's afraid of flying because he's not piloting the plane. He'd choose the predictability of routine over the chaos of surprise because, as he says, "That's how books are made."

What would Quentin—a man who stands perfectly still to make books, whose studio is meticulously clean—look like making a mess in his kitchen? I picture a large room, a goldfinch perched on the bird feeder that hangs from a tree branch outside the window over the sink. Something bubbles in a pot on the stove, and he leans over a cutting board to chop garlic. I can't make out what he's preparing. But I know that if I don't stop visualizing this scene, I'll have heartburn because I feel a space forming inside my stomach and a heaviness dropping into that kitchen-shaped emptiness, and I recognize that Quentin and I will probably never share the act of making a meal. I'm reminded of all the things we can't do together, such as waking up on an ordinary weekday and deciding to call in sick to work so we can stay in bed. Or, on a whim, go somewhere we've never been and get lost, revel in the surprise at what we might discover.

The lyrics of an ad from the late sixties—"How do you handle a hungry man?"—barge into my head and interrupt these otherwise serious thoughts. The singer of the jingle answers his own query with the bravado characteristic of a Western, where you expect John Wayne or Gary Cooper to be the hungry man in question: "The Manhandlers!"

A brand name invented in 1968, when I was still a girl, in response to housewives who asked Campbell's to make a thicker soup for their husbands. Did the person who thought up the Manhandler ever consider that it might, more than three decades later, flash through the mind of a married woman who is not (and never was) a housewife and would never serve soup from a can, and who is uncomfortable being thought of as a manhandler? Sitting across from a man whose mouth and lips and tongue were, only fifteen minutes ago, thick with pleasure and willing to be handled. I sit up straight in my chair and relegate the melody and words to a place in my mind reserved for The Useless Soundtracks We Carry and Play at Random.

What the hell am I doing here? Where are Simone Signoret and Marlene Dietrich? The cheeseburger tastes too good, and I don't want to break the spell, but there's a voice inside me that's saying, "Fold your napkin, get up from this table, and exit the restaurant as gracefully as you can. Go back to your room and cry if you have to, take a shower, reapply your makeup, get out of the hotel, and don't look back." It's not so much the moral dilemma that's at issue here for me, at least not now. I'm more concerned with whether I'm going to become the cliché of a woman who makes herself available to the married man, who makes her wait until she can't wait anymore and then one day leaves his wife. A woman who winds up fulfilling the prophecy I've heard, that married men never leave their wives for the "other" woman, as if that information came out of a self-help book I'd never buy (remaindered at Barnes & Noble), and titled, perhaps, *So, You're Having an Affair with a Married Man?* A guide I'd never use because there are too many variations on this theme, and when you get right down to the reality of the cliché we call an affair, you're still dealing with two people who are entirely different from each set of two people who've ever done this. When I warn myself that Quentin will never leave his wife, my hands feel weak imagining him transforming into a man with a permanent frown and panic attacks that wake him in the night. Or worse, a man who makes the same book over and over

again. I take another bite of my cheeseburger, stop myself from reaching across the table to take Quentin's hand in mine, dwell instead on
the words *beautiful* and *accident*.

Because I feel unable to articulate my internal debate, and maybe
too because I sense Quentin's having a similar one in his own head, I
switch gears. Tell him about the legend of the two giants on the island
of Menorca, where I went in 1979 to sift through dirt and look for
artifacts at the Taula de Torralba archaeological dig. It's my attempt
at impressing him one more time with what he calls my "exotic life."
I know he'll see I'm fabricating a parable. And who knows, maybe
when the fever subsides, when—in spite of what we tell each other
now about loving each other forever—we've become friends who talk
every so often, exchange brief e-mails about our most recent accom-
plishments, and send Christmas cards signed with Xs and Os, he'll
make a book about this legend, his way of announcing across time and
space that his yearning for me hasn't ended.

The two giants, the story has it, competed for the love of a woman.
One built an elaborate well with a spiral staircase inside, and the other
built a *taula*, a table, from two slabs of stone.

"Which giant would you have chosen?" he asks.

Quentin's voice is soft, his smile tentative—not too broad, but
gap-toothed, bemused, as if he's quietly laughing at some joke he just
told himself. He looks like someone you'd need a key to open. But I
can tell—by how he leans forward to listen to me, perhaps, or how
those little lines, delicate as glass shrimp, fan out from the corners of
his eyes, or maybe just because Quentin seems as familiar to me as
my hair—that he knows how I'd answer his question, and he's on the
verge of being sorry that he asked it.

"The one who built the table," I say. *The table we will never sit at
together.*

The waiter fills our water glasses.

"How is everything?" he asks. Quentin and I smile.

We're playing the part of the perfect customers having the perfect meal. No complaints. Nothing out of place, from the real daisies in a vase to each piece of silverware, all of it set just so on the table, as if there were a universal design for flowers and utensils in fancy hotel restaurants. We're speaking in hushed tones, eating at just the right pace; we won't linger too long, nor do we request extra attention or condiments. No one's shedding tears over their cheeseburgers or blowing their noses into the beige cloth napkins. To anyone who might see us, Quentin and I appear as if we're colleagues, acquaintances maybe, having a late lunch and an early drink. Separate checks for the two guests at table nineteen. Everything is fine.

From the neck up, Quentin appears like a man who'd read *Scientific American,* contemplate the shape of pears for hours at the grocery store, drive his kids, then their kids, years from now, to rehearsals and games. To those who haven't been touched by him in ways so reckless that skin will never feel the same; to those who never put their ear to his chest as he sobbed, or tried to imagine how such long, sturdy legs are attached to a man so frightened of failure, Quentin seems like he'll edge his way into fifty sipping bourbon on the porch in summer. A guy who'll never have a surprise party. A man whose greatest terror is that, like ink and paper that aren't of archival quality, he'll fade.

"You know, D . . . ," he starts. He pauses, takes off his glasses, and cleans them with a bandana he's removed from his pocket.

Quentin calls me "D," short for *dolce*; I call him "Q," for *querido.* For a minute I'm afraid he's going to tell me the kissing was great, but it has to end before hearts are fractured irreparably and lives turned so upside down we won't be able to right them again. I want to ask the waiter to dim the lights and make the next drink a double, bring me an ashtray so I can concentrate on the curling smoke of a cigarette instead of the words I'm certain of hearing in the next minute. I promise myself that when I return home, I'll cut off all my hair, ask my papermaker friend Katie to use it in a limited run of paper, and send it to Quentin, who has put his glasses back on and is now dabbing at a bit of ketchup in the corner of his mouth. I rest a hand on the table and stare at my cuticles, which I've obsessively cared for over the last three months, as if my fingernails and the clean, soft bookmaking hands they're attached to might make a difference in Quentin's decision to keep kissing me.

"Only one of those death-row inmates ordered fruit as his last meal," he says finally. "Plums, peaches, nectarines, not cut up or in a fruit cocktail, but whole. You . . . me . . . us, *this* . . . I want it to be like that, like something so different from what anyone else would do in the same situation."

I exhale as inconspicuously as I can.

I want to blame my unprecedented involvement with Quentin on my hormones. After all, they pushed me over enough edges as a teenager, so why not now when I'm on the opposite end of the spectrum, approaching forty-five? As my mother might have said, "Why not blame the things you can?" I tell myself that I didn't plan any of this, that it was Dorrie's fault for dragging me to that reading.

When I told Dorrie that the assistant manager of Barnes & Noble had whispered, "Write me" after we'd exchanged addresses and hugged good-bye, she told me, "You know, Kim, Flaubert said, 'We don't write to live, we write in order *not* to live.' Substitute the word *love* for *write* in that line."

This from a woman so unlucky in love all her friends call her the Queen of Hearts. Yet she managed to flirt with that novelist, even dated him for a couple of months.

Who walks into a Barnes & Noble thinking, *OK, the first married man you talk to, fall in love with him*? Then again, if I had had such a plan, why now? Was I trying to undo the unspoken mandate that yearning should be sublimated, dismissed as an unnecessary ache, a thing one should appreciate as nostalgia for the younger self, a thing that appears in novels or movies? Was I attempting to fall in love so as *not* to live in the vacancies of my life that I thought I might fill by doing something not only out of character but typical of what people do when they're afraid of growing up or growing old? Here is the too-familiar situation of my middle-aged loneliness, probably caused by the depression I'm predisposed to genetically, my failing marriage, and the isolation of living in rural Maine. In Quentin, I find the overused excitement of the illicit—the physical intimacy we're not supposed to have, the shaping of a love that transgresses the boundaries of marriage—which sharpens the heart's response to a world dulled by too many mundane details (think bills to pay, groceries to buy, doctors' appointments, etc.).

If you fall in love with a married man, I've learned, you have to watch yourself be boxed into any number of clichés. Especially if you confide in your friends. And no matter how different you say your experience is, they may respond with a word like *affair,* which grates in my inner ear, an idea I can't invest in because it summons cheap hotel rooms, and makes me think someone's about to brand me *mistress* or *home wrecker.* Or worse, a *manhandler,* uttered with an exclamation point. Implicit in affairs are the things you can't suggest ("Let's sleep in tomorrow morning"), the questions you can't ask ("Are you having sex with your wife?"), and all the things you can't do together (go to the grocery store, hold hands in public, go bowling with friends).

Like Quentin, I want *this* to be different. Already what we're doing feels like an uncharted island—a place we go that's hidden, that we've discovered, and only we know how to find. Not an island where one is held prisoner, but a place of shelter, escape, discovery. There are problems with this analogy, though: islands are fragile ecosystems that erode and shrink, whose shorelines change with weather and water conditions beyond anyone's control. Without bridges, there's only one way to travel to an island, and you might sink as readily as swim. The isolation of an island can transform it into a prison despite any notions one might have concerning the freedom of solitude.

Of course, like acid-free paper and handmade books, I want Quentin and me to last, to be one of those narratives you tell people again and again, the kind that begins "When we first met . . ." or "We knew the minute we saw each other . . ." Yet when I hear such lines, I cringe at how stereotypical they sound. Our story should be bound into a codex, sewn and glued with the breath-holding attention and precision necessary to make a book, a thing that needs stillness and the time to unfold. As I write this, I wonder if I'll have the patience to see it through to whatever conclusion it takes.

The word *cliché* is a printing term from the eighteenth century, designating the plate used for making type. The French verb *clicher* describes the sound of the die striking the metal. It's a shame that this word, which describes a sound I think I'd like—*clee-shay,* a muffled metal *ching*—has come to signify the thing it once produced, the stereotype. Did the printers hearing that noise grow tired of it? Would I?

I've never considered that the clichés I've headed into (including this one) are merely reminders that I'm alive, kicking around the same story over and over, trying to transcend the too familiar, sometimes unable to twist language in new ways to describe what or how I'm living. When I ask Dorrie if she thinks I've trapped myself in a hackneyed situation, she reminds me of her philosophy, that life is one big cliché, with details that make it either magnificent or horrible, or both.

Quentin—no cliché, but a man who has tried to hammer flat his desire, only to find it's still there as a three-dimensional force—plays with a blue-frilled toothpick, the one stuck into my cheeseburger to distinguish its medium rareness. A toothpick I had removed slowly, trying perhaps to accentuate the caution in my fingertips, which were eccentric and careless on Quentin's body only minutes before we sat down to eat. He snaps the toothpick into three pieces, arranges these into a K, whose vertical line is wrapped in blue cellophane.

That toothpick letter is like a miniature colophon, the tailpiece at the end of a book that describes the font used by the typesetter. The word *colophon* comes from the Greek for summit, or finishing touch. The little pieces of wood will be swept away by the waiter after we leave. But for now, that K, splinters protruding on its end and blue on one side, is embossed on the tablecloth, a typeface that will never be replicated.

If Quentin and I are to escape being trapped in a cliché, we will leave our respective spouses, but we won't ride off together into a Hollywood romance that ends on a beach at sunset. In fact, our leave-takings—painful and complicated—will erode the excitement of that first long kiss in the fancy hotel, force it into the shape of a memory whose sharp and exotic taste will dull with time. But before that happens, I'll imagine what it would have been like had Quentin and I been able to fashion a narrative of love in order *not* to live in the inertia of our marriages or the small despairs of our lives. I'll ask him to consider what role I played in his separation and subsequent divorce, to admit that something other than electric attraction sparked between us, a something that warrants honest examination. He will avoid answering my question, and an unmanageable distance will keep us apart. As the time widens between that day in the hotel and some future we've told each other will never occur, we'll think we shared the one and only perfect meal. But eventually, we'll wonder why we thought it so ideal. In time I'll be able to eat a cheeseburger again without the indigestion of regret.

that roar on the other side of silence

If we had a keen vision and feeling of all ordinary human life, it would be like hearing the grass grow and the squirrel's heart beat, and we should die of that roar which lies on the other side of silence.

George Eliot, *Middlemarch*

I. Voices

At the end of the 1990s, I worked at a shelter for victims of domestic violence. I listened to women and their children tell one story after another about how they had fled their own homes. The women spoke of who they once were—prom queens, basketball players, scholarship recipients—and how they had lost their dreams, their selves, their pride. The children, if they spoke, said they loved their fathers, missed their rooms, were afraid of the dark.

I breathed in the silences of what they did not or could not say, the pauses between tears and talk, the unsaid good-byes when they left the shelter—at dawn, in the middle of the night, whenever staff were not present—to return to homes that were familiar but unsafe. I answered the hotline when they called and said they were leaving again—"for good, this time"—and I opened the door to the shelter when they come back, their heads lowered. I raised my own voice to explain—to cops and prosecutors and social workers and clergy and doctors and teachers and anyone whose attention I could enlist—why they "didn't just leave," that they were trapped by economics, family and community ties, and shame. My explanations were passionate and, ultimately, feeble compared to the stories that tumbled from the mouths of those women and children exiled from their own homes.

Once, at the drugstore, I ran into one of the women who had left the shelter and gone back to her husband. We stood at the photo counter. As she retrieved the ticket from her purse, I noticed that the polish on her fingernails was scratched and peeled. Before I said hello, I made sure no one was with her who might question who I was, who might beat out of her an answer.

"How are you?" I asked.

"I'm not dead yet," she said. She raised her sunglasses and revealed black-and-blue circles around her eyes.

But some of them had died or would die and as I walked away from her, I prayed she would leave and go somewhere very far from where we both had met. I realized then I might just as easily have been speaking with the next victim of a serial murderer. The faces and names of anonymous and high-profile casualties began to blend in my mind. Their bruises melded together into a single, giant hurt; their voices tangled as one; and a decade would pass before I could untwine their stories.

II. In a Hotel Room Where Two People Get to Know Each Other
"It's a little bit dark," he says to the woman.

On her knees, she nods. A woman outside herself whose short, thick hair is damp, whose small breasts are exposed. A woman with a string of pearls doubled around her neck and red velour socks that slouch on her ankles, accessories that only serve to heighten her exposure. The light of the city—a blue light from office buildings, the street and its traffic on this moonless night—comes in through the window whose curtain the man has parted. Indigo spreads across the woman's nakedness.

Do you see her? You may be her, I may be her, neither of us may be her. But what if we all were that woman on her knees who waits for the next minute of darkness to descend? She watches the man's eyes for a signal that tells her to hang her head obediently or defy him and face the consequences.

A man stands over a woman who is on her knees, whose hands are bound with the scarf she wore to dinner. He will remove her belt, then his, and he will use them on her flanks. And she will agree to this because she believes there is some kind of truth about trust in how leather and flesh collide. Because they both know he will never buckle his belt without thinking of her, and she will never slide the black leather of hers through the loops of her jeans without thinking of him. Because they know that this belongs to them: the dark, the belt, the bruise.

How would she think or talk about it, if she were to talk about it? She is not sure how to contextualize such a scene. Some might name it pornography, others eroticism. For others, it's called a *lifestyle*. But perhaps it is simply a lesson in something that cannot be properly named, another example of language's inadequacy.

"Are you sure?" he asks. (Do you think he already knows that she is sure?)

She nods, a woman inside herself who looks out, who looks up at a man who has traveled this far, she thinking he never knew he would indulge this desire, he knowing all along he had to assuage it, she a woman outside herself looking in, knowing there is safety in darkness. And not. And too. And yes, she says to her own skin and flesh and heart.

"Yes," she tells him. "I want that, I want you to bring me over the edge into that dark place," but to herself she says, *Don't forget, don't turn back, don't look down, don't blink, don't deny what is happening here.*

His face mirrors how she feels. Reflected in his eyes, in his skin tinted vaguely blue, is a part of them dredged up from that place where they have hidden things. This discovery softens his eyelids (but only momentarily), deepens the crease between his nose and lips, and emphasizes the gap between his teeth. This mask will dissolve for an instant, and when it does, she will see how ugly he might become, how his eyes are hard and almost lashless, his lips thin and dried into a grimace, but she pushes those images from her mind and concentrates instead on the gleam of his eyes, telling herself that in that sheen she sees their mutual wish that he mark her as his. A desire, she thinks, that is entirely separate from how she describes herself—politically accurate where women are concerned, incensed by pornography and violence, able to name any exploitation and get it right. Separate from how she has drawn him in her mind, to justify how he will injure her—a man who respects women, who considers the wrongs made in the name of beauty, who understands how the culture has tricked men and women into roles they'd kill each other to escape.

A bruise will flower on her flesh by tomorrow. As if the light of the buildings, the cars, and the street, in this city where no one knows them, a purplish light seeping through the window well past midnight, has tinted her skin instead of the belt he wields. This exchange of pleasure and hurt occurs in the early hours of morning we erroneously call night, as if there were some clear boundary between one time of day and another, as if we'd forgotten what it was like to be children yearning to trade day for night and night for day, as if we'd never been bruised before.

But she is bruised by his hand, by her belt and his, bruised in trust and longing so old it makes Babylon seem new. And she will wear this mark through tomorrow, and the next day. *Like a medal,* she'll think as she sits, shifting to accommodate that dull ache.

Weeks later he will tell her that indulging their peculiar desire was overwhelming for him. She will wonder if he ever considered her point of view. She'll slip her belt through the loops of her jeans, wind the scarf around her neck, and she'll tremble just a little bit, the mark on her skin long gone.

He will say one thing and do another. The words he utters will include *love, profound, lodge*—nouns, modifiers, and verbs—promises of the abstract habitation she hopes to have set up in his heart. His actions will include contradictions: he'll retreat, not respond, never call. She'll be left hanging, in a limbo where the memory of that blue light exposes her loneliness and her bruise, which is fast hardening into a scar on her stripped psyche. She'll begin to hate him, to wonder why she bothered, and she'll write letter after letter that she'll never send, or she'll try to not call him, hoping he'll wonder what happened, where she is, but calling anyway before she's completed such distancing, unable to cut him off. It's not him she's trying to cut off; it's herself.

And what about him? Have you guessed, that he's already on the trail of the next pursuit, or perhaps he's already taken off his belt for the newest conquest, the one who would explain why he had retreated and was unavailable? For him, one is not enough, and she, our bruised and betrayed woman wearing pearls and socks in the indigo light, is not his first or last. Or second or third. That his appetite cannot be sated. That he is, to put it colloquially, *full of shit.* That she and others in her predicament, in some future time none of them can imagine, will actually say, "What was I thinking? How could I have been duped like that?"

That never, ever, will she say to anyone, "I let him bruise me and I liked it."

III. Genesee River Killer Dies at Sixty-three
We passed them driving home late at night and we cursed them under our breath. They were streetwalkers and we didn't want them around.

They were homeless and they shamed us. When he killed them, we were silent. Someone was cleaning up our community. They were dirt. They were lower than dirt. *Good riddance,* we thought.

When we learned their names—Patricia, Frances, June, Darlene, Anna Marie, Dorothy, Kimberly, Marie, Felicia, and Elizabeth—we felt a little uncomfortable. Those were the names of our wives, our daughters, our sisters, our mothers and grandmothers, our aunts and cousins, our secretaries and nurses and grocery-store clerks and teachers. We never thought of those women he killed as someone's friend or relation. Still, we said nothing.

And then he was caught. He had returned to the scene of the crime. It was January. The body of this last victim was frozen. The police arrested him. We showed outrage when we learned he had killed two children before he came to our city and murdered those prostitutes.

We listened to the news of his trial. We wanted to believe that he couldn't help himself, that he did what he had done because he was brain injured, had suffered abuse during childhood, and went to Vietnam. We wanted to believe that the kind of hatred implicit in his crimes was impossible, though at moments—especially on Friday and Saturday nights, when we worried about our own children who stayed out too late—we knew, even if it was only for a passing second, that such hatred is not only impossible, it's like a virus. We despised those women too.

Now he's dead. We are older; some of our daughters have run away and are on the streets; some of our friends are homeless; some of our relations are bruised. Some of us are more tolerant now. Some of us speak up now, even if only to whisper the names of the dead in prayer.

IV. In the Shelter for Battered Women

Women arrive here bruised. Some with emotional contusions you can feel across the room and cannot see, some with all variety of blue, brown, russet, and ocher marking their skin. Around the eyes where he's hit her. On the arms where he's grabbed her. On the buttocks where he's kicked her. On the neck where he's tried to choke her. On the knees when he demanded that she beg for mercy, for the dog's life, for the safety of her kids. For her life.

Children arrive bruised: wrists and ankles, the back, legs, and face. And deeper still: their child hearts and livers and kidneys and spleens and lungs and stomachs. And deeper yet: their child genitals, still hairless most of them, still waiting for something gentle to happen there.

If you worked here with these women and these children, you might go home and make a mental inventory of injury. You might do this every night (and if you've never prayed formally, you might begin to confuse this exercise of reviewing the hurt of others with a kind of prayer). There's Carla with two black eyes and Jane with asthma and insomnia and irritable bowel syndrome and Alice with a busted rib and Gina with a nose broken twenty times and Sally with clumps of hair torn out and fingertips bloody from where she's chewed them and Ellen, so quiet you suspect her vocal cords were damaged when her boyfriend—she actually called him her *lover*—tried to strangle her.

You will get nervous about whether they are safe at night in the shelter (its location is confidential, but everyone knows where it is), not just from the husbands and boyfriends and partners and fathers and brothers who inflicted the bruises, but with themselves, with each other.

Consider Elaine, a woman in her late thirties, with her bleached-blonde hair showing its roots and her creased face that makes her look like she's almost fifty, the one waving the knife as she speaks, the one who nods when you tell her she can't use drugs or alcohol while she's staying here (under the beneficent eaves of the state-funded, federally mandated safe house), who has her stash and her dealer ("I give him head, he gives me a nickel bag," she'll announce later in blatant disregard for the rules), and besides, she's a grown woman, and who are you to tell her she can't snort a line or smoke a jay or down a shot of tequila? And then there's Angie, the mother of two who will abandon her three-year-old daughter and try to cross the Canadian border with her infant son, a young woman who has lived in communes and on the streets of New York City and in shelters from Florida to Maine, whose hair is now red but probably started out brown, who cuts herself regularly, favoring the soft flesh of the belly, a part of her body she reveals whenever she can. And who can forget Tanya, the overweight ten-year-old who pees on the floor and throws such violent tantrums no one can restrain her. Or Bobby, the toddler who knows how to get what he wants by smashing his hand in a face—his mother's, his infant sister's, yours even.

And there's the Ojibwe woman whose nickname is Cricket, who has four kids, the oldest of whom is anorexic and darkly beautiful and so sad there should be a law—not the flimsy kind of law already in place, but a law that truly prevents all this damage from being inflicted. If you look into this woman's eyes, you'll start to understand why they call her Cricket, that it's not a reference to some cute cartoon bug with a top hat, but a name that evokes her potential to summon the fearsome sound of ten thousand crickets trapped in your living room and wanting to leave. You will fully understand this when you hear her scream, hear her voice lift up and out of her (like a beacon, or maybe, you'll think later, the sound of a demon) when the social worker from Child Protective Services, accompanied by a cop, orders you to open the door so they can take away Cricket's children because, says the social worker, Cricket has *failed* to protect them. You may have trouble understanding how Cricket has failed since she did, after all, leave the scene of too many crimes and come here, finally, to this shelter, even if she mentioned that she wants to go home. They all want to go home. The social worker does not mince words. And though she doesn't say it, you can feel her need to rush this transaction. She knows a nice family waiting to adopt a baby boy, this baby boy whom Cricket will not relinquish. By the end of the day, the whole family will be fractured, Cricket's three girls ferried off to separate foster homes, places where no one speaks Ojibwemowin and where no one checks to make sure they're being fed and clothed and bathed. The older one will perish quickly, falling through a crack so wide you'd need a truck full of concrete to fill it in. She'll be abused in foster care, she'll run away, she'll be caught, she'll turn eighteen and be freed from the system, and in ten years, when she is the age her mother is now, she'll call the shelter hotline and then open this very door through which the social worker and the cop are waiting to escort her now. As this hour of your life passes, this travesty of justice, this wrongness, the police officer keeps shaking his head and telling you and the rest of the staff that he wishes he were anywhere but here. Every time you think of Cricket, her bruises—especially the ones you can't see—will grow larger. You will never forget her kids, the oldest locked in the bathroom with her two sisters, the baby crying, Cricket holding him tighter and tighter, sobbing and begging the white social worker for a second chance, the social worker saying over and over again that Cricket is making this *transition* more difficult than it has to be, the cop outside the locked bathroom door talking the oldest girl into unlocking it, you helping the two youngest girls throw their meager belongings into a black garbage bag. And when you ask the youngest of the sisters if she knows what's happening, you'll see her stare into a place past any heart, a place that chills you just to think of it. Later on this evening, the children gone and the shelter quiet, Cricket will tell you how she's going to fight to get those kids back and you tell her you'll help, but she'll be gone in the morning, no note, no forwarding address, and you will feel what it's like to fail to protect someone. Several months later, you'll learn that she's in jail for soliciting; Cricket will not see her kids until they are grown and she is older than she ever imagined. She will become an aged and ragged Cricket, her loveliness hidden beneath tattered clothes, discarded with the leg lost to diabetes, buried beneath skin sallowed by cigarette smoke and too few days in the sun.

Late at night, as you catalog their faces and names, their ailments and idiosyncrasies, their lives and loves gone sour, you'll remember that all you can give them is the promise of acceptance, which means that all you can do is listen, telling them, when the time comes, that they don't deserve the bruises they've sustained. This small assurance is so very tiny, especially when you imagine what you might do if you could take all the money used to keep the shelter in compliance with the ten thousand rules imposed by the state and the feds and give it to Carla and Alice and Jane and Gina and Sally and Ellen and Elaine and Angie and Tanya and Bobby and Cricket.

V. Like a Woman Sitting in an Empty Chair

What would happen if one woman told the truth about her life?
The world would split open.

    Muriel Rukeyser, "Käthe Kollwitz"

Dear Muriel,

When the world splits open, I hope you will catch me when I slip through.

Every time I tell people the story of how my husband treated me, I can feel them thinking, At least he didn't hit you. *The truth: I wish he* had. *You get hit and it's over. A bruise results; there's evidence. And once the fist has made contact with flesh, the cycle reaches its peak, even if it happens again and again. You see that fist coming.*

In my world, there was no peak, there were only constant eggshells under foot. . . . I'd set the table and come into the dining room to discover the place settings removed, or wake in the morning to find the contents of the kitchen cabinets rearranged, all the cupboard doors left wide open. Gifts I placed under the Christmas tree for my two sons would disappear. Not one day passed when I wasn't called stupid. "You're going crazy," he'd tell me, every night before bed. The words seeped into my dreams and distilled them into nightmares. I became afraid to fall asleep, to dream worlds in which boxes of cereal and saltcellars and cans of soup would grow legs and faces and arms and march out of the kitchen past me, giving me the finger or spitting at my feet. Once in a nightmare, all the frying pans exploded and the grease splattered me everywhere.

He'd tell me I said things I didn't remember saying: "You called Mrs. James a hag when we went to the PTA meeting; you told our neighbor you were going to dye your hair green. Why do you say such things? You probably have Tourette's." And then he'd tell me I had forgotten saying all this, that I probably had early Alzheimer's too. He'd glare at me when the breakfast I cooked wound up in the trash, though I hadn't put it there. "You're going crazy. Maybe I should commit you," he'd say. And then he'd make me get completely undressed and cook a new breakfast: bacon, crispy, and eggs, over medium. I'd have to stand there and watch him eat. And when he was done, he'd put his plate on the floor and make me get down on all fours to scarf up the crumbs and lick the egg yolk. He forbade me to read, to watch television without him, to make phone calls. He never allowed me to drive anywhere alone. We lived at the end of a long road and had no neighbors. Most weekends, he'd take the boys to his camp in the woods, but not before emptying the kitchen, leaving me with only a big box of saltines and a case of beer and instructions to finish them both. He'd turn off the water and shut off the electricity and record the numbers from the meters so if I dared turn them on again, he'd know. I suppose there was always the threat he'd hurt me physically, and that fear was worse than if he had simply hit me. As it was, I developed sleeping disorders and an ulcer and I lost weight and my hair started coming out in clumps and by the time I finally left him, after thirteen years of marriage, I was malnourished, had stopped menstruating, and was a nervous wreck.

One day, I packed a small bag and walked out. I couldn't believe how easy it was, even though I was scared and I didn't want to leave the kids like that, with him. I went to the shelter. They were nice to me. They even helped me get into a place of my own. Transitional housing, it's called. Because, I guess, you're making a transition from the unreal world to the real one. The thing is, living in that house, as nice as it was, I started to go crazy for real. I heard his voice telling me he'd find me, telling our two sons that I'd abandoned them, telling the police I needed to be locked up. Each night, I'd check the cupboards and fridge and draw pictures of where everything was. I'd check them again in the morning. I became obsessed with doing this. I saw doctors. They gave me Valium and Xanax and sleeping pills and antidepressants, but nothing eased my nerves. I'd dream of him breathing on the back of my neck. Awake, I was always looking over my shoulder, expecting him to be behind me. One day, I couldn't take it anymore, so I took all the pills. If it wasn't for the nice lady from the shelter, who came in that day to bring some new curtains, I'd have died on the kitchen floor. After that, I wasn't allowed to stay in transitional housing. I went back to the shelter. Eventually, though, I found my own apartment. I was hired as a receptionist in a health center. People there looked out for me. They gave me covered dishes of good food. They called to make sure I wasn't alone too often. They helped me find a free lawyer, who worked with me to get custody of my kids, something I thought I'd never be able to do since I believed I really was crazy. I joined a group of women, and we talked about what had happened to each of us and, just like everyone kept saying, I realized I wasn't alone. But sometimes, instead of comforting me, it made me very sad, that so many women had these stories. Still, I started to get better. After two years, I gained some weight and even had my hair colored and cut. I bought new clothes, the kinds of things he never let me wear, like V-neck sweaters and skirts. People told me I looked good. My lawyer had advised seeing a therapist, that it would help my case. I learned I wasn't crazy after all. A social worker came to visit me every week and although I was afraid of her at first and the reports she was writing, eventually she told me that I was as fit a mother as she'd ever seen and she recommended to the judge that I be granted custody. The day before the hearing, my husband called me at work. "Insane people can't care for children. I'm going to kill you," he said and hung up. I went into the bathroom and cried so hard my mascara ran all over my cheeks and when I looked in the mirror, I saw the face of a crazy woman and I cried until I vomited and vomited until I retched and retched until I was drained. When I went back to my desk, I felt like a woman sitting in an empty chair.

Finally, I was divorced and my sons came to live with me. The oldest, who was fifteen, was very angry. He tried to push me down the stairs. He repeated the kinds of things his father used to say to me, and I was scared of him. But I persevered. I found help for my son. I felt solid working a good job and having my boys at home. I even had friends. I wasn't going to let anyone take me away from this new life.

On the first-year anniversary of my divorce, they found me in my bedroom, with a shotgun positioned between my knees. Everyone thought my death was suspicious though eventually it was listed as a suicide and the case was closed. "Women rarely use guns to kill themselves. She was too short to have used that gun," the state police officer in charge of the investigation told the district attorney. My ex-husband had a foolproof alibi. But my oldest son, he was home when I died. The theory of the crime was that his father talked him into shooting me and setting things up to make it look like I took my own life.

No one but me is sure how I died. And I don't want to tell you because either way—whether I committed suicide or was killed by my own child— neither of us was guilty. Either way, I was murdered. And my husband, he never laid a hand on me.

Respectfully yours,
One Woman Telling the Truth

nine segments of orange

Change the code.

George W. Bush, February 7, 2003

I.

I started worrying about the meaning of the color orange the first time a Code Orange Security Alert was announced in September 2002. As the news focused on the possibility of war, and then the invasion of Iraq and the war itself, I felt as if I were encountering orange for the first time. I pictured thick smoke released in explosive puffs of dark ocher. I contemplated buying a gas mask.

Code Orange. In the sequence of security-code alerts, orange signals the threat of danger as "high," between the "imminent" of red and the "elevated" of yellow. The middle child of the three warm colors in the revised American rainbow, where indigo and violet are absent, and blue comes before green. Blend red and yellow and you get not only orange but a certain ambiguity folded into the advice on how to prepare for unpredictable acts of danger.

Code Orange. I listened to the advisories to stock water, canned food, and enough duct tape and plastic sheeting to keep one designated room free of pathogens or particles. I read the Red Cross suggestion to review my "personal disaster plan." I vacillated between wondering if I really should have bought duct tape and plastic, or if

I should have written a letter to the editor entitled "Duct Tape and Plastic, Who Are They Kidding?" I made mental notes to fill some water jugs while sending blessings to my nephew, who was then stationed in Afghanistan. Before falling asleep I took a silent inventory of the canned food in the cupboards. I should be doing this anyway, I told myself. Before the war began and the code was changed back to orange, and all during its yellowness—the failed diplomacy and the mobilization of force, the dragging on of violence—I started to feel anxious thinking of orange.

How did we get here? Can I refuse this new definition of orange?

II.

In "Why I Am Not a Painter," the poet Frank O'Hara declares:

> . . . There should be
> so much more, not of orange, of
> words, of how terrible orange is
> and life.

When Code Orange was announced a second time in February 2003, I thought I finally understood what O'Hara meant by "how terrible orange is." Before that moment, all I had ever really thought about orange had been condensed into a sentence I often repeated: "Orange is a color I appreciate only in nature."

There was the full moon rising on the pale shimmer of a winter solstice, how it arced over the horizon. A molten annunciation of all things orange, from pale apricot to fiery vermilion.

There were the goldfish and carp that mesmerized me with the chiffon swish of their orange tails. Monarch butterflies and the web of velvet black stretched over the dark-orange-dusted wings. I considered cantaloupe, papaya, mango, and the tropical rhythms of their names. The peppery surprise of a red-orange nasturtium in my salad and the buttery slip of calendula petals. The papery trumpets of squash flowers and the Chinese lanterns of tomatillos. The dark amber maple leaves of autumn.

"Of how terrible orange is *not*," I wanted to say to O'Hara.

III.

I would not be surprised to learn that cosmetic and paint companies employ haiku poets to develop the names of their products: Coral Serenade, Shy of Shrimp, Pearled Peach.

Imagine if these poets wrote the handbook for national color code advisories. Imagine Code Curry—an invitation to share food, to use red, orange, and yellow as levels of spiciness instead of hierarchies of alert. On Code Curry days, we would welcome the stranger to our tables and feast on all the foods that symbolize abundance. Pomegranates, carrots, sweet potatoes, honey.

IV.

When I was a little girl, my friend Libby and I liked to perform short plays and songs that we had composed. I remember the first line of one of those songs: "Orange," we sang. "I saw the sun come up this morning . . . orange." It was likely each of us had seen more sunsets than sunrises, but the idea of dawn—and the challenge to write a song whose words didn't rhyme—captivated us.

I'm still curious about mornings. I like to wake up to the dark, fuzzy orange of 5:00 AM. The scent of an orange being peeled on a winter day reminds me that awakening is both pungent and urgent.

V.

Though I still prefer orange in its natural incarnations, its artificial versions have also shaped my penchant for the frivolous and absurd. The orange, for example, in foods I no longer eat—Creamsicles,

Cheese Nips, and Orange Crush—but whose familiarity somehow anchors me.

There is the oddly comforting shock—perhaps because I recognize O'Hara's orange in it—from 1970s America, of orange shag carpets, electric orange plaid RV interiors, and orange polyester. I was a teenager when I first listened to the band called Tangerine Dream and experimented with the LSD known as Orange Sunshine.

The orange of my coming of age was too sweet, too loud to be camp, too experimental. While it was not quite bad enough to be good, it was mine.

VI.

The artifice of orange seems more serious now. Suddenly I notice it everywhere, demarcating different social boundaries. The Dial deodorant soap that purports to silence our primal scents. Surveyor's tape tied to trees. Traffic cones announcing accidents or detours. The alert of fluorescent hunting apparel. Prisoners working on the roadside.

I reflect on all that is terrible about orange and see the danger O'Hara saw. Anita Bryant, the auburn-haired beauty queen, telling us that a day without orange juice was like a day without sunshine and then going on to trash gays and lesbians (and the poetic justice when the Florida Citrus Commission ended her contract). The British import of fear called *A Clockwork Orange* (and the real-life terrorism it inspired, not to mention the moot debate on whether life imitates art). Agent Orange, exported to poison the Vietnamese and their land. Golden Rice, engineered with beta-carotene to nourish people whose once nutrient-dense soils have been destroyed by imported chemicals.

In Crayola's Giant Chest of Crayons, I find *atomic tangerine* and *neon carrot*. Who named these colors and where do they buy their produce? What orange secrets do they know?

VII.

I don't want this new definition of orange. I don't want to associate it with the gray, damp blandness of duct tape and plastic sheeting, bottled water in the basement, canned food. I don't want orange to mean fear.

"The world," writes Gabriel García Márquez in *One Hundred Years of Solitude,* "is round, like an orange." When I read this sentence, I knew I wanted to tell stories. When American armed forces were first dispatched to Iraq, it was this orange I clung to: a dimpled ball, full of potential to be sweet, juicy, fragrant. In its segmented flesh, I see a metaphor for storytelling; its rind and seeds spin parts of speech into the narratives of a world.

At first, the *terrible* of O'Hara's orange made me think of the awe you feel in front of something so ordinary—a piece of fruit or a story—that you must, if you are a poet or a painter, capture what you sense as extraordinary.

VIII.

My friend Rachel, who is both painter and poet, once made a drawing of all seven chakras in the trunk of a tree, seven spirals of color from red to violet. An orange coil represented the second, sacral chakra, where our energy is described as belonging to water, and expresses sensuality. This energy center, situated in humans an inch or so below the navel, is also said to be responsible for clairsentience, clear feeling.

I imagine Rachel blending all the oranges of her experience— from the yolks of fresh farm eggs to jack-o'-lanterns glowing on October nights—to conjure in that whorl of energy the entire spectrum of orange's complexity.

Not long after she made that drawing, Rachel wrote a poem, in which she imagined "orange blooms of lichen on the dark bodies of whales." When she utters it, *orange* never sounded so good. It is as if the color gurgles in terra-cotta mud and emerges with the elegance of marmalade.

IX.

If I had to safeguard only one image of orange, it would be a photograph I made of dunes in the Sahara Desert on a March day in 1986. Unlike the ambiguity of Code Orange, the ambiguity of this photograph delights me. Turn it upside down, and you could be looking at a painted landscape, flat hills scalded blue at sunrise or sunset. Turn it vertically, and you might see an orange thigh at twilight, or the cobalt curve of a tree trunk at daybreak.

It's not an exciting picture: no shadows, no apparent subject, no real attention to composition. What I like in this image is how the orange sand bumps up against the blue of late afternoon to proclaim the emptiness of heaven and earth. So entirely empty that it is full. Implied in that vacant landscape of sand is a collective of particles; examined close up and individually, they are like the dots in a pointillist painting, ranging in color and transparency from melon to carnelian to rust. But together these grains express a unified orange with a singular tone and texture. If I could touch it, it would feel like adobe warmed by the sun.

I remember standing in that desert, feeling the immensity of orange, its hot beauty and extreme thirst. The picture that remains conveys an orange that mutes what O'Hara saw as inherently terrible and preserves the awe of something as everyday as sand.

This is the orange I desire, the one I want to think about when our president—the one I didn't vote for or elect—leans over to another guy in charge and says, "Change the code."

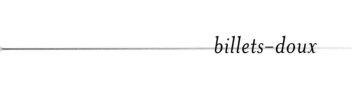

billets-doux

intersection

I stand at the corner of Lexington Avenue and Eighty-seventh Street in New York City, an intersection I crossed hundreds of times for three years on my way to school, *hundreds of times,* I think, more than thirty years ago. I no longer live here, but I can visualize the girl I was—at this intersection and this crossing—how she waited diligently for the light to turn green, looked around, and assumed the act of crossing, a book bag on her shoulder and hips that swayed just enough. As if getting across the street were as involuntary as blinking. She believed then that such movement would be as much a part of her physical self as the nails on her toes. It was practical to think that here was the life she knew, so why would it change? There were no plans yet to move out of the city and into suburban New England where she never fit in, nothing about being hijacked out of a place she loathed then desired once she left. She could not foresee the thousands of miles she would clock, the different rooms she would open her eyes in, all the dishes she would handle. She never considered how she might intersect with other people, the many tears that would fall, the insomnia she would suffer, or what time would do to her body. No one had looked at her palm and told her what it means when life and love intersect. She wasn't thinking then about how she would stand in some future at hundreds of other intersections and cross them almost as boldly, or as carelessly perhaps, as she was crossing this street on her way to school.

I stand at the corner and call you from a pay phone. Behind the words I utter, a mix of noise issues from trucks and taxis, the pedestrian shuffle, and the murmur of cell-phone conversations, each one a variation on the same themes of love and work. The smell of roasted chestnuts wafts from a vendor on the corner. I want to tell you how much I love chestnuts, their odor of almost bread but sweeter, the little paper bags they're packed in, and how when I lived here, I ate them as I roamed the city's streets. How the chestnuts warmed my hands in winter. How I used to forget those bags, full of chestnut shells, in a pocket, and how my coat then smelled of charcoal and sweet toast. Instead I talk about sledding in Central Park with my father when I was a kid. Your voice is in another state, and between the soft-volume pay-phone connection and the rush of the avenue, you sound so light I think for a second that I'd be able to lift you, an impossibility when we stand face to face and gravity contains us. You say, with a tenderness that could drop me to my knees, that you want to hear more about me as a kid with my father for a father.

As we talk, I wonder what people may hear as they pass me, my head turned into the metal hood around the phone, my cheeks getting windburned anyway, my ear pressed into the receiver. What one word drifted past the man with the briefcase stepping into the street to hail a cab? Will he remember it? Use it later in another sentence, out of context?

No one has come looking for me here, but I feel her eyes on me. That young girl pauses at the intersection and shakes her head. *Surely,* I can feel her thinking, *surely that can't be me when I'm older. Surely when I grow up, I won't look like that.* What is it she does not recognize? Perhaps all she sees is a woman leaning into her right hip with a smile that is tentative and outrageous at the same time, a forefinger poised on her upper lip, talking into a pay phone on the corner of Lexington Avenue and Eighty-seventh Street.

I ought to be crossing the street, the girl thinks. *I ought to be . . .* What she cannot articulate yet is that she should consider the future, or how to intersect with more grace and less cleverness, or how to turn around at particular crossroads and forgo crossing altogether.

Just then, as you and I are disconnected because of some glitch in the pay phone that doesn't let us talk more than twenty minutes at a stretch, as I'm pulling out your phone number and the phone card and negotiating paper and buttons with one ungloved hand, the handset precarious on the slip of my scarf and collar, I catch a glimpse of that young girl. I look up and she's looking at me and I'm looking at her look at me. At the same moment we are looking back, we both realize that although she sees a woman with desire as long as the avenue and wide as the street, a woman wishing she still had that girl's body (but not the tangled mind), she—the girl—is the one who doesn't belong here. She hasn't traveled this far yet. Though she hasn't dropped her foot off the curb, she's still in the middle of crossing the street, dreading the math test today, hoping she'll be desired by a boy she knows, and completely unconcerned with any event beyond lunch. A small paper bag full of chestnut shells in her coat pocket.

She knows, however, that something is different here and now, at odds with every other day she has crossed this street. For an instant so brief it could be contained in a particle of soot, she senses through her toes the points of connection between these streets and that woman on the phone. She vaguely understands that she may be setting her foot on the other side of time, the place I stand now looking back at her.

full green jacket

Her traps—some as subtle as a mink at night, others as obvious as a grackle—wake you in the night. Even Seneca knew that going to bed is not restful, that darkness does not slake the thirsty mind, it only "gives us a change of anxieties." Since you never talk about the banalities and frustrations that keep you awake (the bills you pay, how indifferent she is to your dreams, why she never empties the dishwasher), you lie there instead imagining the flowers colored buttercream, cotton candy, shell white. She has dresses of these colors in the closet, dresses she will not let you wear, though she has worn all of your clothing. You reach over to touch her dark curls, the hair you've braided and loved, a trap that now captures the moonlight coming through the window. Her breathing is deep and slow, and like the promise of her beauty, it is another snare. You listen instead to the constant swell and drain of the ocean on flat sand—tide in and out, out and in—the forever of flux. The sky stretches wider than albumen, the clouds synchronized to the breath of each tree leaf, immune to the arguments about intimacy and money, and the implication you sense in those disputes that you should support her brilliant career and ignore yours.

In the morning, you slip into the full green jacket of summer to ward her off. You pretend to take shelter under the cool mantle of earth that belches forth lupine, iris, hydrangea. You tell her that too much heat gives you a headache. The dogwood, wild pear, and apple blossoms have gone by; you wish that last argument had departed with them. The lupines she planted are so heavy they bend to the ground as if purple and pink were not colors, but magnets pulled toward the earth's core. You don't dare pick them.

You need a different apron this hot summer day when the sink is piled with dishes, the towels lie crumpled on the floor—an insinuation hovering in the air that you pick them up, wash, dry, and reshelve them. She's been swimming and has eaten lunch and is showered, wrapped in a white robe watching television. You try to shower, but there are no more towels, there is no more hot water. You are hungry, but she's finished the peanut butter, the tuna fish, all the bread. You imagine being swaddled in a green that drips and weeps in the afterbirth of every burgeoning fruit, every young animal. You tell her, "We have to talk." She switches the channels, catching a minute here and there of every permutation of every love story, ignoring yours.

The memory of her loveliness—skin glabrous like that of a porpoise, thighs like those of a boy, the way she purses her lips before choosing exactly the right word—traps you. The recollection of before—you are living in after with her now—lodges between your teeth, pushes into the gum line, provokes infection. The more you try to dislodge it, the more resolutely ensnared it becomes.

You yearn for the regularity of heartbeats transient and shy: dragonflies, the ever-present brown-to-white-to-brown-again rabbit, coyote even. She tells you that you are depressed, but what's really happening is that you have no more patience for fighting. You are more interested in the soft noises coming from the woods, a fox paw perhaps, or the papery sound of feathers. Because you know what an expert she is with traps—how, for example, she'll offer to listen with you for those discreet movements in the forest, reciting the true names of the birds and the ancient stories of the wild dogs—you tell her you want to be alone when what you really want to do is leave.

You start to conceal things from her. Like the woodcock in the backyard. "Little lovers of the swamps and bogs," they were once called. Shy birds with long beaks whose markings mirror the spongy earth on which they set their delicate feet. You watch them, their feathers patterned like dead leaves, as they shuffle in the underbrush, pulling up earthworms. The "little language that lovers use," Virginia Woolf wrote of the communication that begs to remain in its primordial state, ungrammared and undeclined. Whole. Never translated or broken in meaning. The little language you speak with her is now fat with declension, bound by the rules of usage, gagged by the passive. You resolve to have that talk with her, the one she avoids at all cost, even though it is easier to collect secrets, to make up stories about the little lovers in a swamp.

She never wants to take the time to undo the effects of the razor syllables you have both learned to speak. It is easier for you both to watch the remains of life *in aqua* surface at low tide. Broken bits of shell—blue-pearled mussel, ivory moon snail, bleached-bone sand dollar. What was once whole and moving on its own under water is now fragmented, protruding, sharp. These shards could cut open your foot as sure as glass, and you suspect she is unwilling to walk back to the house for the peroxide and bandages. You imagine a scenario where you do not bleed to death but get gangrene instead. A doctor tells you he'll have to amputate your leg. The nurse keeps asking why you didn't come to the hospital sooner.

You practice the art of camouflage, blending in with the scenery. A raggedy red fox pads out from the edge of beach grass to snatch something from a pile of seaweed and retreats into the periphery. She sees the fox, brazen in broad daylight on a beach full of people, and declares its danger. It could steal babies, she says, or their souls, and while she rages at its potential for heartless thievery, you silently congratulate it for its blatant survival.

It is becoming more difficult to listen to the silence that widens between the talk you need to have and never start. Instead you train your ear on the constant bass twang of bullfrogs. If the tiger lily were an instrument, it would be a horn. Playing a mandarin orange riff about July from tall roadside grasses and cultured lawns, urging us to pay attention to this royal month. You try to tell her this but she cannot hear you. She tells you she has an ear infection. You tend to her, caressing her hairline as she leans on a pillow and you squeeze drops of medicine into the tunnel of her ear, one by one. And you know that no amount of nursing will bring that inner ear back, the one she lost, the one she might tell you was stolen by a fox.

A sour odor wafts out from her mouth whenever you get too close and overwhelms the fragrance of raspberries in a bowl on the counter. She begs you to tell her why you no longer touch her. You try to explain that you cannot provide the intimacy she craves, though the truth is that you came to feel repulsed and overwhelmed by the smell of decay on her breath. Not alcohol or tobacco, but a very old wound—a mother who beat her as an infant, a stepfather who raped her sisters, her inability to protect them—that she thought was preserved in the dry ice of her memory and is now putrefying. What comes out of your own mouth is a lie, wrapped in the feverish stink of your ambivalence, your hesitance to dissolve, once and for all, the trap of her regal beauty. You turn your nose instead to the baked-grass smell of summer heat, like the straw hat you gave her that she left in the sun.

Not even mid-July and the blueberries have come. You once picked them together, fingertips brushing in a bramble. You and she stood together on the barrens, feet bare against the brim of the earth's sweet salt sweat, clover simmering alongside almost-ripe raspberry, the odor of fur, feather, and shell. The shimmered flight of a dragonfly. The threads of the full green jacket of summer in your hair.

others of your kind

For Eleanor

Imagine learning to howl. You set out on this adventure with an idea in mind about hunger. Your goal: explore that hunger; learn about it so intimately that you can summon a growl from your stomach.

But first you need to learn to use your eyes. Specifically, you need to know how to win trust from others by using the blink, the turned head, the averted gaze. Your eyes: cast elsewhere. Submission precedes the relief from hunger, something inside you whispers. Or so you think. This is merely something you know, in the same way you sense how things in the range of your world work.

You practice using your eyes. You involve your eyebrows, the lashes, of course, the I'm-smaller-than-you look of vulnerability. You invite compassion, or at least persuade the two-legged ones who feed you into a Momentary Instance of Sympathy. (It could be Empathy, but you're not sure.) It works: the bowl is filled. You sate your hunger. You eat quickly, an instinct.

You learn that patience precedes food. But you also remember the old ways, when your days and travels were determined solely by hunger, when your nights were guided by the passage above of a light that changes shape each night, over and over.

When that light is a whole perfect circle, you feel the need to howl.

It is another kind of food you ask for when you howl, not the solitary bowl placed on the floor, but the invitation to the communal gathering, hunting, and feeding. An announcement of hunger.

Because of this patience-for-food trick you've learned to do with your eyes, or maybe because you sleep near the two-legged ones who feed your kind, you have forgotten how to raise your nose to the air and push out the hunger in one long single syllable.

Imagine then learning to howl. Not the hidden belly groan. Not the sweet yodeling some of your cousins use to delight the two-legged ones. The pure howl, nose like an arrow piercing that round white light in the dark sky, the sound pulsing forward from the end of your tail, a sound that splits open all conversation and lets the others of your kind know you are near.

Imagine learning to howl. We set out on this adventure with an idea in mind about hunger. A group of women at night. Full moon. Someone wonders aloud what it would be like if we howled together.

We sit in a circle. Each of us has come from a different place and time to arrive here, at this moment when we howl together. We have all learned some lesson about hunger, submission, the use of our eyes in the theater of vulnerability. We all know about the involvement of eyelashes, the variations on passion.

We have sated hungers not necessarily our own. We have held so many bowls in so many ways we cannot count them all. Right now the only bowl we covet is the moon, and we will hold it by learning how to howl.

We are impatient. We barely remember the old ways so we retell them to each other. We raise our faces to the sky, to the bowl, and push out the hunger in one long single syllable.

Imagine learning to howl. Not the hidden belly groan of our own unsated hunger. Not the sweet yodeling we have performed to plea-sure others. The pure howl, mouth open like a bowl to the sky, the sound pulsing and radiating forward from the pelvis, a sound that splits open all conversation and lets the others of your kind know you are near.

two teacups

Gettysburg, Pennsylvania, 2007

I.

They were nested snug in a black box fashioned of thick cardboard. The kind of container that says "sturdy," with a heft that endures. On the cover of the box, he had taped the letters of the word *writers*—cut out from a magazine, in no particular order, a constellation of white letters dancing on black.

It reminded me of the ancient rabbis, who wrote the holy words in honey on a slate. "Lick them off," they instructed their students, "to remember that language is sweet."

II.

These cups have no handles, perfect for warming cold fingers. They are small enough for my hands. In the candlelight of gift giving, the soft brushstrokes of glaze on their rims look like blurred moths.

III.

Care for these teacups, protect them from breakage. Wash them by hand after all the other dishes are done. Hide them away before the house sitter comes.

IV.

I cannot be someone's secret, not ever again.

Stand on the mountain and tell the stars that the way of beauty is as strong as black tea, that in me you taste sweet jasmine and spiced ginger, that together we drink the laziness of oolong, the urgency of pekoe, that you found me when we needed each other most.

V.

It is not because of desolation or loss that I came to this love.
It is because you knew these cups were made to warm my hands.

VI.

Some years ago in a loneliness, I drank myself into a stupor, out cold by six. I did not hear the phone ring. I woke at nine, made some tea, smoked a cigarette, took a sedative. I was shaking and shivering and could not stop. Every part of me ached.

I sat at the kitchen table and held my teacup in both hands, watching the moths outside flit under the light, but nothing erased the deep edge of night, or the cold; nothing softened the ache.

When I returned to bed, the sound of my own expelled breath woke me before I had fallen asleep. I could have sworn someone was standing close enough to breathe into my exposed ear.

Startled, I rose from the bed in the darkness, avoided stepping on the cats, who had—as cats do—positioned themselves on the stairs, tried to call out for help, but my throat was too dry and I knew no one would answer.

At that moment I hated what I had done to get through the darkness of my day, the poison I had ingested, how ineffectual it was, how costly the price of my passage through a solitary night.

VII.

Tonight, and still I cannot sleep. The writer's teacups are in the cupboard, the kitchen dark save for the ribbon of street light that spills through the space between the curtains, onto the linoleum. The house is chilled, as empty as the bottle of plum brandy on the shelf, a bottle that will one day hold the single orange rose you have not yet given me.

Waves of passing headlights wash the ceiling. I weigh your words, consider the conditions I have no choice but to accept if we are to drink together from these two teacups.

It's no big deal, I think finally, after the pillow soaking and nose blowing, the grief that congests. *There is nothing anyone has that I need anymore.* I know that's not true, but I try to believe it.

VIII.

First light tumbles through the gold curtains in the living room. I open the cupboard. The teacups nest snug on the shelf.

"If you let me," I whisper to the morning, "I will love you for a long, long time."

i just lately started buying wings

Her voice, like some holy place, issues from a warm brown prayer of a face. She's going blind. She doesn't worry about her son's alcoholism anymore, or the injustice of the everyday.

"It's like lye in the sink and you better not put your hands in it," she says.

She'd know. She's cleaned a lot of houses. Put her hands into a lot of sinks in other people's homes.

"You ought to get married, Annie," she tells me. I don't know why she calls me Annie, but I've always liked it. She tells me that her niece's two kids are on drugs and can't get off, and how her sister's grandson was shot and killed. I shake my head.

"I'm not ready to get married," I say. I tell her that my brother is still on drugs, and my other brother, dying of AIDS, is also still using. She shakes her head.

Believing as I do in the power of food to blur the distinctions that keep people hungry, I ask her if she would mind very much telling me her recipe for fried chicken.

"I ain't ever told nobody how I makes chicken. I tell people how I makes cakes," she says.

We talk and talk. I will not press her for the fried chicken recipe, which, like her exact age, is one of the few secrets she still maintains.

She rubs Nivea lotion into the keen flesh of her tightly muscled calves. These legs have carried her to homes where she has made the dailiness of other people's lives a little more bearable. Legs her own son held on to as he learned to walk (her son, now a man who lives alone somewhere in Baltimore, who drinks too much and doesn't stay in touch). Legs that carried her to the work of feeding and cleaning and raising other people's children. She has the legs of one of those saints who walk among us unnoticed. Legs of sustenance for which we should thank God, the Creator, Vishnu, Allah—whatever we believe in— each and every day.

She says the trip home to her sister's in Virginia Beach is too much this year. She says she's mad at those doctors who lie to her, and the trip into the city is too long to see those lying doctors. She says she's thinking of getting a new place, one with an elevator.

"Stairs, Annie, is getting hard on my old legs."

Her vision, she reminds me, is like the weather. "On clear days, I sees like lightning." On rainy, cloudy days, everything is blurred. She tells me the A&P on Flatbush Avenue is only two bus stops away, a beautiful market, but she buys her meat at the butcher shop, where she can smell it. She relies more on her nose these days.

"I like the breast, the short thigh," she says. "But, Annie, I just lately started buying wings."

As she says this, I think of her ascending on splendid wings that navigate the places she can no longer walk to or see. Wings of soft brown, darkening to bittersweet chocolate at their tips.

Then, she tells me her recipe for fried chicken:

"Don't put nary a drop of salt because those seasons are salty. After I wash my chicken, I take paper towels and dry it. Then I put on the season. It's very important to put your season on the chicken before you flour it. If you're not a good flourer you can put it in a paper bag, or a plastic one. But it's very important on your season. Don't put no thyme on fried chicken. Don't put no sage on fried chicken. I use a little papriker and a little bit of Lawry Season Salt. Then I use a little Acćent. Acćent's very important to it, the chicken. And I use white pepper, not black pepper, just a dash. It's better to put the season on a half hour before you flour. Use Crisco oil. You can use Mazola, but I use Crisco. You have the pan half full with oil, and not lukewarm. You fry it with a cover and a long fork. And you don't turn it over and over. Just turn it when it's crisp on the edges."

When she's done speaking, she rocks in her rocker, hands loosely clasped in her lap. We sit in silence, the secret she has spoken floating between us as if it were a feather.

see me slant:
poetry considers her mother

Poetry ought to have a mother as well as a father.
  Virginia Woolf, *A Room of One's Own*

I am a woman who slants. Standing, I lean into my right hip. When I catch myself doing this, I realign, redistribute my weight, and establish that poise my mother would be proud of, standing as if a book were balanced on my head, my neck full of understated attitude, my eyes focused on an object across the room, hips symmetrical. My mother insisted that I practice this posture, the dictionary resting on the crown of my skull, shoulders fluid, my gait as smooth as suede. I'd cross the room several times as she watched, and this practice always occurred in silence, as if spoken words might topple all that vocabulary just above my head. Whenever we went out in public together, my mother, taller than I, would bend slightly and whisper, "Stand up straight."

My mother gave me this body, the one that slants while standing, and she worked hard to ensure that I'd have a voice of liquid amber for those words that teetered on my head, along with the common sense to pause and rearrange myself when aslant. She gave me practical advice—where to dash, how to shape my nails into commas, what style to wear, whom to date, when to use a period. And when I was older, my mother instructed me in the art of reading between the lines, and how to catch—as if they were fireflies—the words that live in the mind. She showed me how to care for my lips so they'd be useful, and how to keep my tongue clean so as not to disturb the ecology of what I tasted.

I grew up in my mother's body. On the long, wide savanna of her back, I pretended to be grass. In the fertile crescent beneath her breast, I hid like a turtle. At the twin beaches of her thighs, I invented waves. I browsed in the orchard of her hair. Found safety in the coves between her toes. She offered me these landscapes connected to her body, along with a universe beyond—the constellation of her mind and the momentum of her orbit. She could fold herself into a boat simply by wrapping her arms around me. My mother was all these dimensions at once: the place of arrival and point of departure, the act of journey, the vessel that affords passage, the North Star that guides.

As a child, I listened carefully to my mother, watching her mouth as it shaped what it uttered, imitating how she touched her lip in a coy-mistress kind of way as she hesitated to locate the perfect word, my ear against her chest as she fashioned a sentence out of thin air. She was always leaving language around the house for me to find, asking me to celebrate ordinary things like fish houses or oranges, and to consider extraordinary ideas like the design of an oyster or the curve of time or the progress of a beating heart.

My mother divided time into stanzas. Matins we sang to the breaking day and last vestiges of starlight. Before lunch, we'd wash windows and banish the dust, setting the house in order like any mother and her daughter. She showed me how to organize the bureaus into sonnets, folding fourteen articles of clothing mixed in color and utility into each drawer. How to iron out the wrinkles and sew on the buttons. Afternoons, we would paint haiku on the bathroom mirror, and look at our reflected faces webbed in the seventeen syllables of our design. At twilight we cleaned our pens, repaired the spines of books, and my mother would hum a tune for the rising darkness. It was always at this hour, the moment between day and night (the hour when a wolf might be mistaken for a dog, as they say in French) that she would rest her teacup on the table, lean toward me, and tell me things she knew. Like the true names of the birds. Or that each person I encountered would be as full of stories as the great library rumored to have stood at Alexandria. That she named me Poetry to keep her body alive, a fleshy dialogue across the ages.

After dinner, she would open all the doors and windows in the house and I would explore. She always hid something for me, in the closets or the attic, under my bed, in the medicine cabinet. A moth wing. A swatch of black velvet. A lead pencil. A bell jar. A copy of *National Geographic* from 1918. A wild iris. A blackbird feather.

I started my exploration in the house, sometimes running from room to room, sometimes standing still and closing my eyes, focusing my entire inside self to divine where she had hidden the latest treasure. After I located and studied the gift she had secreted away, we would stand in the frame of the front door, my mother and I, until she stretched her arms out to the night.

"This is your backyard," she always said. "Play in it all you want, but come home when you're ready."

I learned to see in the dark this way, to stand so still that I could hear a spider repair its web, smell the breath of trees, sense the dance of water murmuring beneath my feet. Sometimes I held my tongue out, trying to catch a solitary raindrop. When it snowed, I took off my shoes.

As I grew older, I yearned to hold hands with the darkness, to shape it into a person whom I could bravely face and tell my secrets. I longed to build a house of night for my secret keeper, a dwelling that smelled like moss and safety where we might lie down as lovers and tell each other stories until daybreak. There I would sit, alone in the geography of desire, summoning a human form with a human heart, remembering to choose each word as if the wrong word at the wrong time might dissolve my lover's hands. I was never ready to go home, never tired of playing this game.

My mother knew that I would not return once I wandered in the place she had invented for me. She did not want me to be nostalgic for her, for our house, for the gifts she left me.

"That was the point," she always said. "That you'd become a cartographer, that you'd know how to come home even if you didn't want to."

She was an expert at redefining and expanding desire's boundaries, pushing me against that uncomfortable edge you must navigate to reach clarity. Because my mother was expansive in imagination, I was able to steer beyond the melancholic pulse and the cynical wink, and out into the land, not to be silenced as some have been silenced who move into the world, but to make it part of memory's biography. Infuse it with images and sounds and that invisible thing in the gut that falls through the center of the body when one is alarmed or aroused, stunned or stunning.

The day she died, my mother reminded me to care for memory as if it were my child.

"No tarrying too long in the backyard," she said.

But I could see the coy-as-a-coy-mistress smile (something my father had inspired in her, I am sure) tugging once again at her lips, and I knew she was not completely serious. I believe she was telling me instead to take all that I remembered with me, as if it had a hand I could hold, a body I could love, the acuity to rename everything possessed of a beating heart.

When I lean into my right hip, it is as if I were trying to lean into another body, place my head on its chest. Sometimes I feel the heat of a torso, the bone of the hip, an arm, like the secret keeper I made of night in the topography mapped of my mother's body and mind. And often I hear its voice.

"Stand up straight," it always says.

With thanks to James Baldwin, Elizabeth Bishop, Laure-Anne Bosselaar, M. Wylie Blanchet, Mark Doty, Louise Glück, Jane Kenyon, Phillip Lopate, Andrew Marvell, Frank O'Hara, Sylvia Plath, Wallace Stevens, and Virginia Woolf.

publication acknowledgments

"Anatomy of My Father" was originally published as "Paved with Good Intentions" in *Hotel Amerika*, 6.1 (Spring 2008).

"Four Points" appeared, in a different incarnation, in *Quarter after Eight*, volume 10 (2003), and was the recipient of the 2003 Robert J. DeMott Prose Prize from Ohio University.

"Habeas Corpus" was originally published in *Ninth Letter*, 4.1 (Spring 2007).

"I Just Lately Started Buying Wings" was originally published in *Brevity*, #21 (Summer 2006).

"Intersection," "Full Green Jacket," and "Others of Your Kind" were originally published together as "A Short Grammar of Love" in *Hotel Amerika*, 5.1 (Fall 2006).

"Nine Segments of Orange" was originally published in the *Louisville Review*, #58 (Fall 2005).

"The Perfect Meal" was originally published in the *Baltimore Review*, 9.2 (Summer 2005).

"Pregnant Madonna Scrubbing Floor" was originally published in *Alaska Quarterly Review*, 23.1/2 (Spring/Summer 2006).

"Relief" was originally published in *Hotel Amerika*, 3.2 (Spring 2005); reprinted in *Best American Essays 2006*, ed. Robert Atwan.

"See Me Slant: Poetry Considers Her Mother" was originally published as an *AGNI* Web exclusive in April 2008, and reprinted in *Fourth Genre*, 11.1 (Spring 2009).

"Teeth in the Wind" was originally published in *River Teeth*, 7.2 (Spring 2006).

"That Roar on the Other Side of Silence" was originally published in *Hotel Amerika*, 8.1 (Fall 2009).

"Two Teacups" was originally published in *Alimentum*, Issue 6 (Summer 2008).

"Wings over Moscow" was originally published in *Cimarron Review*, Issue 155 (Spring 2006).

acknowledgments

I am grateful to Sue Halpern for selecting this book for the 2009 Katharine Bakeless Nason Prize in Nonfiction. Many thanks go to Michael Collier and Jennifer Bates at the Bread Loaf Writers' Conference for all their hard work.

Singular appreciation goes to two extraordinary writers who are also master teachers (and, I'm lucky to say, good friends): Barbara Hurd and Michael Steinberg read almost all the essays in this book more than twice and were tireless in their efforts to raise the bar. In a past lifetime, Marcia F. Brown, Joan Connor, and Jim Sprouse were my companions on quixotic quests; in this lifetime, they enliven and enlighten my days. For the past eight years, I have had the great good fortune to enjoy laughing, kvetching, and learning with Penelope Schwartz Robinson and Sarah Stromeyer, whose love, wisdom, and generosity of spirit are without measure. The poets of Heimlich House—Tracy Bozentka, Marcia F. Brown, Michelle Lewis, Jo Solfrian, Eleanor Steele, and Elaine Webster—contributed to the conviviality of a communal living space, comforted me, and persisted in assuring me that I was onto something. All the people I've just thanked would be strangers to me if not for Lee Hope, who brought us all together with her vision for the writerly community of the Stonecoast MFA Program.

Friends in Washington County, Maine, where many of these essays were hatched, helped me pursue my writing in many different ways. For appreciating and telling stories, a big *woliwon* to all who welcomed me at Sipayik, especially willow and her grandson Dakota, Virginia Aymond, Cyril and Dute Francis, Nancy Soctomah, and Alice Tomah. For attending to the well-being of Cobscook Bay, on whose shores I contemplated many of the ideas that found their way into this book, I am grateful for Cathy and Terry Bell; Rachel Bell and Sam Furth and their children, Finn, Inez, and Jonah; Jim Dow; Alan Furth; Will and Elizabeth Hopkins; Katie MacGregor; Pat Mallar; and Suzanne Plaut. I am also thankful for the encouragement from Robert Froese, Bill Prescott, and David Rosen.

Praise goes to the oft-unsung editors in the world of literary publication who shepherded these words into print: Marcia Aldrich, Robert Atwan, Sven Birkerts, Polly Carden, Matthew Cooperman, Dinah Cox, Jean Cunningham, Susan Muaddi Darraj, Steve Davenport, Katie Dublinski, Jenny Dunning, Hayley Mitchell Haugen, David Lazar (whose two cents are worth gold), Paulette Licitra, Joe Mackall, Karen Mann, Fiona McCrae (who read this manuscript three times), Adam McOmber, Dinty Moore, Sena Jeter Naslund, William Pierce, Peter Selgin, Lauren Slater, Terence Smyre, Ronald Spatz, Jodee Stanley, Michael Steinberg, and Catherine Taylor.

Thanks to all the folks and fellows at the Virginia Center for the Creative Arts, and many thanks to Jack Ryan, Peter Stitt, and the staff of the *Gettysburg Review* at Gettysburg College for supporting my time there.

I am blessed with a circle of family and friends, who have taken time to read and respond to what I write, engage me in provocative conversations, and/or simply shelter me in their kindness: Magda Aboulfadl, Michelle Auerbach, Beth Blevins, Leslie Borden, Corrie Calderwood, Sarah Davis, Peter Deutsch, Leone Donovan, Mark Drew, Kris Driscoll, Stephen Dunn, Michael Edwards, Peter Engel, Steve and Joan Engel, Kelly Bennett Freeburger, Holly Grant,

Laurie Jane Hayes, Rachel Herzig, Richard Hoffman, Natalie and Jack Holtzman, Sandra Hyde, Jodi Lerner and Bob Freeland, Pat Madden, Patti Maxine, Rebecca McClanahan and Donald Devet, Suzanne Menghraj, Louise Mirkin, Cheryl Perko, Melissa Rigas, Joan Rosenbaum, Mimi and Stu Schwartz, Heather Simons, Lochlin Smith and Marietta Rhyne, Trellan Karr Smith and Dan Taylor, Suzanne Strempek Shea, Marilyn Springer, Becky Welsh, Rick Wile, Dorrie Wilson, Iris Yellowcloud, and Paul Zimmer. I couldn't have finished "Habeas Corpus" without the assistance of public defender number one, Rick Greenberg. Roberta Gordon, my oldest friend and one of my many sisters by choice, not only reads everything I write, she has stood by my side, no matter what.

This book would never have happened without the lightning-edged spirit of Dustin Beall Smith, who provided me passage to a new world when he opened his heart to me.

Finally, I send blessings to all the people, living or passed on, who appear in these essays—without them I'd have fewer stories to tell.

Bread Loaf and the Bakeless Prizes

The Katharine Bakeless Nason Literary Publication Prizes were established in 1995 to expand the Bread Loaf Writers' Conference's commitment to the support of emerging writers. Endowed by the LZ Francis Foundation, the prizes commemorate Middlebury College patron Katharine Bakeless Nason and launch the publication career of a poet, fiction writer, and a creative nonfiction writer annually. Winning manuscripts are chosen in an open national competition by a distinguished judge in each genre. Winners are published by Graywolf Press

2009 Judges

Linda Gregerson
Poetry

Percival Everett
Fiction

Sue Halpern
Creative Nonfiction

Kim Dana Kupperman is the recipient of the 2009 Katharine Bakeless Nason Prize in Nonfiction, selected by Sue Halpern and awarded by the Middlebury College Bread Loaf Writers' Conference. Her work has appeared in many literary periodicals, including *Best American Essays, Fourth Genre, Hotel Amerika, River Teeth,* and others. She is the founder of Welcome Table Press, a nonprofit independent press dedicated to publishing and celebrating the essay, and she works as the managing editor of the *Gettysburg Review.* Kupperman lives in Gettysburg, Pennsylvania, and New York City with her husband, Dustin Beall Smith.

I Just Lately Started Buying Wings is set in Arno Pro, a face designed by Robert Slimbach and named after the river that runs through Florence. This book was designed by Ann Sudmeier. Composition by BookMobile Design and Publishing Services, Minneapolis, Minnesota, and manufactured by Versa Press on acid-free paper.